Buying Real Estate Foreclosures

Melissa S. Kollen

McGraw-Hill, Inc.

New York   San Francisco   Washington, D.C.   Auckland   Bogotá
Caracas   Lisbon   London   Madrid   Mexico City   Milan
Montreal   New Delhi   San Juan   Singapore
Sydney   Tokyo   Toronto

Library of Congress Cataloging-in-Publication Data

Kollen, Melissa S.
    Buying real estate foreclosures / by Melissa S. Kollen.
        p.   cm.
    Includes index.
    ISBN 0-07-035817-6 :   — ISBN 0-07-035818-4 (pbk.):
    1. Real estate investment.   2. Foreclosure.   I. Title.
HD1382.5.K65 1992
332.63'24 — dc20   91-22214
                                                    CIP

        8 9 0   DOC/DOC   9 7 6

ISBN   0-07-035817-6
ISBN   0-07-035818-4   {PBK}

*The sponsoring editor for this book was David Conti, the editing supervisor was
Caroline Levine, and the production supervisor was Suzanne W. Babeuf. It was
set in Baskerville by McGraw-Hill's Professional Book Group composition unit.*

Printed and bound by R. R. Donnelley & Sons Company.

Buying
Real Estate
Foreclosures

For Steve—My Best Friend, My Inspiration,
and the Love of My Life

and

For Jimmy—My Special Pride and Joy and the
Wealth of My Life

For Mom—My Biggest Fan, My "momager"
and the Foundation of My Life

Contents

List of Sample Forms, Illustrations, and Checklists

Introduction

Buying Real Estate Foreclosures was written to provide the reader with the necessary tools for the successful purchase of real estate foreclosures. But before we get into that, let me first commend you for taking your first steps toward achieving these goals. By choosing real estate in general, and foreclosures in particular, as your vehicle to success, you are joining thousands of entrepreneurs who started out just as you are now—with a dream and the motivation to attain it.

The vast majority of people use their money to buy furniture, furs, jewelry, and other luxury items. But in five years, will a $5000 living room set be worth more or less? The answer, of course, is less. Entrepreneurs are different. We want more. We will forego immediate gratification for future gain, so we look to buy real estate, which will be worth *more* in five years.

How many of you have bosses who stay up late at night thinking of ways to help *you* make a lot of money? On the other hand, how many of you have worked diligently for others, for many years, and made *them* a lot of money?

You will never get ahead by waiting for a boss to give you what *you* think you deserve. You have to achieve for yourself and you must take control of your own destiny. Whether you are a renter who is looking for the Great American Dream of homeownership, or an investor who is looking to build wealth, the information contained in this book will help you to achieve your goals.

Now, I am *not* going to tell you that little effort is involved in buying foreclosures. Everything worthwhile in life takes *some* effort. But the ratio of effort involved to success generated makes foreclosure purchasing incredibly worthwhile.

Who Would Be Interested in This Book?

This book is designed especially for the following types of readers, re-gardless of their experience level, occupation, financial status, or state of residency:

Renters who long for the Great American Dream of homeownership at affordable prices.

Investors who wish to purchase properties at below-market prices.

Real estate professionals who wish to help customers buy foreclosures and who want the knowledge offered in this book for consulting pur-poses.

Contractors who want to buy a foreclosure that needs work, make re-pairs to it at minimal costs, and either keep the property or sell it for a profit.

Entrepreneurs who wish to build wealth by utilizing foreclosure con-tract transfers for a profit.

Accountants who wish to help clients obtain foreclosures as a tax shel-ter.

Attorneys who want to help clients with creative ideas for avoiding foreclosure, and who need to understand the procedure and the available options.

Parents who want to help their children get a head start by owning real estate, and who are curious about creative new techniques that will benefit everyone involved.

Landlords who wish to turn negative cashflow into positive cashflow and avoid tenant problems.

The list is seemingly endless.

Why This Book Is Unique

I began in real estate over a decade ago—buying, selling, renting, man-aging, and creatively financing hundreds of real estate properties. When I first began, no information was available to help get me started. It was hit or miss, and thankfully, I didn't make a lot of mistakes—at least, not more than once! I wanted to make it easier for those who are following in my footsteps. With this in mind, I have written a hands-on guidebook based on my own experiences. Therefore, this book comes from the heart. I have been in the trenches. I have had the same questions, doubts, and feelings of inadequacy that many people feel when they try something new. I conduct seminars on the subject of buying foreclosures, as well as other real-estate-related topics, that are attended by thousands of people. In my seminars and in this book, my goal has been to stimulate people by implementing easy-to-follow procedures toward acquiring foreclosures. Along the way, I have sprinkled in some of my own real-life experiences. By using this method, I hope to instill in people the confidence needed to reach their goals.

Of course, there are other books on the market that deal with the subject of investing in foreclosures, but this book is unique for several reasons. It prepares the reader to buy foreclosures using practical, street-smart techniques. It explains potential roadblocks (such as unfriendly occupants and missing legal documents) and gives proven, practical methods for dealing with uncomfortable situations.

The book is geared to *all* levels of experience. Beginners will appreciate the step-by-step procedures and checklists for buying foreclosures, which are presented in easily understood language. Experienced buyers can also make effective use of these lists, and they will appreciate having the procedures laid out for them in a clear-cut, logical manner. Beginners will appreciate the explanation of various financing options. And experienced buyers are always looking for new financing ideas, and they may very likely find a method here that they hadn't thought of before. Beginners and experienced foreclosure enthusiasts alike are always looking for new sources where they can find foreclosures, along with the procedure they will need to follow to bring the purchase to fruition. Beginners will appreciate learning about any potential problems they may face *before* they make costly mistakes. Experienced buyers will appreciate "war stories" which they can relate to and learn from. They may have already encountered some of these drawbacks, and they will benefit further from new ideas that can save them (or make them) money in the future. And even if an experienced foreclosure purchaser has not yet encountered any of the problems I have mentioned, they will now have been made aware of and will be prepared for them in the future.

Finding What You Want

The topics in this book have been organized in the following manner:

Legal procedures. The legal procedures behind a foreclosure action are explained to provide readers with an insight into how a foreclosure procedure progresses when a lender forecloses on a delinquent borrower.

Characteristics of foreclosures. The characteristics that make foreclosure purchases different from a typical property purchase are identified so that the reader can see both the benefits and the risks involved.

Buying foreclosures *before* the auction. The benefits of finding, approaching, and negotiating with delinquent homeowners before they are foreclosed on are uncovered and explained.

Buying foreclosures *after* the auction. REOs: The benefits of finding and negotiating with the most motivated sellers of all.

Buying foreclosures at the auction. A typical day at an auction is described as are the procedures for buying a foreclosure at an auction, including what to do, what to expect others to do, and the step-by-step procedures for bidding on a property, from inspection through closing.

Finding foreclosures. Readers are given eight major reference sources where they can locate or obtain lists of available foreclosures, including government agencies, in every state in the Union.

Financing foreclosures. The reader is brought behind the scenes of a mortgage application situation to learn money-saving tips that are used when comparing lenders. Readers are also presented with creative techniques for financing foreclosures with little or no cash.

Choosing the property that is right for you. The step-by-step procedures for choosing the right property and calculating an offer or bid amount are described.

What to do when your offer is accepted. The steps to follow when you are the high bidder at an auction or when your offer is accepted for a foreclosure are detailed.

What to do when you are the new owner. The procedures to follow in preparation for foreclosure ownership are discussed.

Getting started today. Everything is tied together so that the reader can begin to put all of the information he or she has gathered into practice.

Other Major Features in This Book

1. Ten innovative methods for financing foreclosures with little or no cash.

2. Nineteen magic questions to ask to help distinguish a dream from a disaster.

3. Hidden additional costs to expect when buying a foreclosure.

4. How to get free real estate property values.

5. How to approach unfriendly occupants and get past the guy with the pit bull and the shotgun.

6. A lifesaving safety tip.

7. Six steps to take to turn your dreams into reality today.

8. Sample copies of legal documents involved with foreclosure purchases.

9. Worksheet for calculating your personal bid sheet in order to avoid "auction fever."

10. Form letters calculated to help open the doors of delinquent homeowners.

11. Offer letters to send banks for REOs.

12. Letters to cooperative and uncooperative occupants living in the foreclosure you want to buy.

13. Easy-to-use checklists include: procedures for bidding, steps to take after the contract and after the closing, and the magic questions for determining the true value of the property.

Melissa S. Kollen

Acknowledgments

I would like to gratefully acknowledge the following people for their efforts on my behalf. They have supported this project with unlimited contributions of their time, advice, and expertise.

David Conti, my publisher at McGraw-Hill, whose belief in me and my ideas has turned a lifelong dream into reality.

Olga Wieser, my agent at Wieser & Wieser, for her encouragement and kindness, and for always being there.

W. Adam Mandelbaum, attorney, for sharing his legal expertise in all phases of real estate and foreclosures.

Tom Caulfield (Suffolk County Title Insurance Co.) for contributing so much of his time and support and for sharing his expertise on the many intricate aspects of title work.

Katherine Spears (information specialist, Resolution Trust Corporation, Office of Communications) for her invaluable assistance and insight into the workings of the Resolution Trust Corporation.

The following people have helped me tremendously with their expertise in financing practices in general, as well as with their insights into a lender's view of bank-owned property: Robert DiBella, Green Point Savings Bank; William Holihan, Citibank, NA; Ray Ludwig, Long Island Savings Bank; Eleanor Cutlar, The Dime Savings Bank; Tom Riccobono, Norstar Bank.

Walter Eidelkind (Long Island Realty Co.) for providing the setting for where it all began, the "golden keys" to unlock the doors, and the opportunity to use them to the best of my potential.

George Wexler, C.P.A., for his guidance and expertise relating to financial and investing matters.

Stuart Stein, attorney, Certilman, Balin, Adler & Hyman, for his contributions on the legal aspects involved with foreclosures.

John Reno, attorney, Reno & Arturo, for his expert counsel and advice on landlord-tenant legal matters.

Martin John Yate, author, for the gift of his friendship and for easing my path through the doors of the literary world.

Taucher-Chronacher, Professional Engineers, P.C., for invaluable assistance in the art of building inspections and for allowing me to use portions of their forms for illustrative purposes in this book.

Jay S. Turner (TICOR Title Insurance) for assistance with deeds of trust.

Mr. Steffeck (HUD) for his efforts, advice, and invaluable information about HUD sales and FHA foreclosures.

Mr. Rooney (VA) for sharing the procedure involved in purchasing foreclosures from the Veteran's Administration.

Joanne Von Zwehl (RDA Enterprises) for her enduring support, ongoing encouragement, and many contributions from an investor's viewpoint.

Sandra Yankowitz (Real Estate Consulting and Training Co.) for holding down the fort while I met my deadlines.

A special thanks to my mom: All my life you told me I could, and therefore, I did. Thank you for your endless loving support. And dad: Your faith in me is a special driving force.

Buying
Real Estate
Foreclosures

1
Understanding Foreclosures

The Basic Foreclosure Procedure

Each state and county in the United States has its own specific procedures for taking foreclosure action, but the *basic* principle is the same everywhere.

In a foreclosure, a mortgage lender may legally reclaim possession of a property if the borrower has failed to make an agreed upon number of regularly scheduled mortgage payments within a contractually specified time frame. As an example, let's consider a mortgage document that stipulates that a mortgage will be considered in default once the borrower, or homeowner, is 90 days late with the monthly mortgage payment.* The mortgage balance at the time of default was $90,000, and the borrower's monthly mortgage payment was set at $1000.

After missing the first monthly payment, the borrower owes the regular $1000 monthly payment plus late charges. And after missing a second monthly payment, the borrower owes $2000, or the equivalent of two monthly payments, plus the late charges. But, once the borrower misses the *third* monthly payment, the mortgage's due date becomes accelerated, that is, it is *due now,* and the borrower owes *$90,000,* or the

---

*In this book, the terms *delinquent borrower* and *delinquent homeowner* are used interchangeably because within this context they are, in effect, synonymous.

full mortgage balance, plus the late charges. The borrower is no longer permitted simply to pay off 3 months of overdue payments. The lender is now legally entitled to "call" the mortgage, which will require the borrower to pay off the entire principal balance due.

At this point, the lender may opt to sell the property at an auction to be held at a designated location. If such is the case, the public is notified according to local custom, usually through advertisements published in the local newspapers. A referee will accept verbal bidding to purchase the premises on behalf of the foreclosing lender, and the contract will be awarded to the highest bidder.

Mortgages and Deeds of Trust

The foreclosure procedure terminates those rights that the owner of the property had secured, either through a *mortgage* or a *deed of trust*. Both mortgages and deeds of trust are legal instruments that create a lien against the property. When the borrower defaults on the loan agreement, the lender can sell the property in order to satisfy the balance of the outstanding loan obligation.

The United States is about equally divided in the use of deeds of trust or mortgages as the security system used for mortgage loans, and a few of the states even use both. Figure 1-1 lists which systems are used in each state. Figure 1-2 is an illustration of a deed of trust, and Figure 1-3 is an illustration of a note and mortgage.

Mortgages and trust deeds contain wording that explains what will happen should a borrower default on a loan. Let's take a look at the differences in foreclosure procedures for a mortgage and those for a trust deed.

A Mortgage Foreclosure

In those states that use a traditional mortgage loan system, when real property is mortgaged, the borrower must sign two separate instruments: the *note,* or *bond,* which is evidence of the promise to pay the debt, and the *mortgage,* which is the legal instrument that creates the lien on the property as security for the debt. The *mortgagor* is the borrower, and the lender is the *mortgagee.* If the mortgagor, or borrower, fails to make payments, then the lender has to take some action. Depending on its policy, the lender will usually send a letter advising the borrower of late payment and requesting that the mortgage payment be made immediately. If the payment remains in arrears, many lending in-

Figure 1-1. Mortgage loan systems used in the United States.

State	System used
Alabama	Mortgage
Alaska	Deed of trust
Arizona	Deed of trust
Arkansas	Both
California	Deed of trust
Colorado	Deed of trust
Connecticut	Mortgage
Delaware	Mortgage
District of Columbia	Both
Florida	Mortgage
Georgia	Mortgage
Hawaii	Mortgage
Idaho	Deed of trust
Illinois	Deed of trust
Indiana	Mortgage
Iowa	Mortgage
Kansas	Mortgage
Kentucky	Both
Louisiana	Mortgage
Maine	Mortgage
Maryland	Both
Massachusetts	Mortgage
Michigan	Mortgage
Minnesota	Mortgage
Mississippi	Deed of trust
Missouri	Deed of trust
Montana	Deed of trust
Nebraska	Deed of trust
Nevada	Deed of trust
New Hampshire	Mortgage
New Jersey	Mortgage

(Continued)

Figure 1-1. (*Continued*) Mortgage loan systems used in the United States.

State	System used
New Mexico	Deed of trust
New York	Mortgage
North Carolina	Deed of trust
North Dakota	Mortgage
Ohio	Mortgage
Oklahoma	Mortgage
Oregon	Deed of trust
Pennsylvania	Mortgage
Rhode Island	Mortgage
South Carolina	Mortgage
South Dakota	Mortgage
Tennessee	Deed of trust
Texas	Deed of trust
Utah	Deed of trust
Vermont	Mortgage
Virginia	Deed of trust
Washington	Deed of trust
West Virginia	Deed of trust
Wisconsin	Mortgage
Wyoming	Mortgage

stitutions will still try to contact the delinquent borrower. The lender wants an explanation for the nonpayment, as well as an opportunity to try to work out a plan to bring the mortgage current. If the mortgage cannot be brought current, or if the delinquent borrower is uncooperative, the lending institution will turn the action over to its attorney.

In most cases, the attorney will look at both how far behind the borrower is with current payments and how timely all previous mortgage payments had been. If the attorney is unable to work out a payment plan with the borrower, he or she will proceed with the foreclosure action on behalf of the lender. A *foreclosure search* will be ordered. This is a report from a title company that gives the attorney information about

2402
Prepared by the State Bar of Texas for use by lawyers only.
Revised 10/85; 12/87.
© 1987 by the State Bar of Texas

DEED OF TRUST

Date:

Grantor:

Grantor's Mailing Address (including county):

Beneficiary's Rights
1. Beneficiary may appoint in writing a substitute or successor trustee, succeeding to all rights and responsibilities of Trustee.
2. If the proceeds of the note are used to pay any debt secured by prior liens, Beneficiary is subrogated to all of the rights and liens of the holders of any debt so paid.
3. Beneficiary may apply any proceeds received under the insurance policy either to reduce the note or to repair or replace damaged or destroyed improvements covered by the policy.
4. If Grantor fails to perform any of Grantor's obligations, Beneficiary may perform those obligations and be reimbursed by Grantor on demand at the place where the note is payable for any sums so paid, including attorney's fees, plus interest on those sums from the dates of payment at the rate stated in the note for matured, unpaid amounts. The sum to be reimbursed shall be secured by this deed of trust.

Trustee's Duties
If requested by Beneficiary to foreclose this lien, Trustee shall:
1. either personally or by agent give notice of the foreclosure sale as required by the Texas Property Code as then amended;
2. sell and convey all or part of the property to the highest bidder for cash with a general warranty binding Grantor, subject to prior liens and to other exceptions to conveyance and warranty; and
3. from the proceeds of the sale, pay, in this order:
   a. expenses of foreclosure, including a commission to Trustee of 5% of the bid;
   b. to Beneficiary, the full amount of principal, interest, attorney's fees, and other charges due and unpaid;
   c. any amounts required by law to be paid before payment to Grantor; and
   d. to Grantor, any balance.

FOR ILLUSTRATION PURPOSES ONLY. REPRODUCTION PROHIBITED.

Forms may be obtained through State Bar of Texas (512) 463-1463

Figure 1-2. A sample deed of trust.

CONSULT YOUR LAWYER BEFORE SIGNING THIS FORM—THIS FORM SHOULD BE USED BY LAWYERS ONLY.

NOTE AND MORTGAGE

$..................................   Date..

Parties   Mortgagor

               Mortgagee
               Address

**Promise
to pay**
principal   Mortgagor promises to pay to Mortgagee or order the sum of
amount (debt)   dollars ($
interest   with interest at the rate of   % per year from the date above until the debt is paid in full.
payments   Mortgagor will pay the debt as follows:

**Application
of payments**   The Mortgagee will apply each payment first to interest charges and then to repayment of the debt.

**Address
for payment**   Payment shall be made at Mortgagee's address above or at any other address Mortgagee directs.

**Transfer of
rights in**   **Additional promises and agreements of the Mortgagor:**
the Property 1. The Mortgagor hereby mortgages to the Mortgagee the Property described in this Note and Mortgage. Mort-
                gagor can lose the Property for failure to keep the promises in this Note and Mortgage.
Property   2. The Property mortgaged (the "Property") is All
Mortgaged

FORMS MAY BE PURCHASED FROM JULIUS BLUMBERG, Inc.
NY,NY, OR ITS DEALERS. REPRODUCTION PROHIBITED.

Figure 1-3. A sample mortgage.

the owner, the mortgage holder, and other creditors who have an interest in the property, including any second-mortgage holders, lien holders, mechanic's lien holders, judgment holders, utility companies, and holders of federal and state tax liens, and property tax liens.

At this time, the attorney usually files a *lis pendens* (notice of pending action) with the clerk of the court in the county where the property is located. The *lis pendens* gives notice to the world that the lender has brought about an action to foreclose on the delinquent borrower. Once the *lis pendens* is filed, any additional liens or judgments against the property will not be included in the foreclosure action. After the attorney files the necessary documents with the courts, all parties named in the action (creditors, tenants of the owner, trustees) must be served with the mandated foreclosure papers. Some states require that the delinquent borrower be served within 30 days of filing the *lis pendens*. If the delinquent borrower has a tenant residing in the property that is being foreclosed, then that tenant must be named as part of the action or the successful high bidder may have to abide by the terms of the current lease that exists between the delinquent borrower and the tenant, even after the successful bidder becomes the new owner.

The mortgagor has a time limit within which to respond to the complaint issued by the lender. If no response is made, then the lender's attorney will submit a report to the court stating the facts of the case and requesting that the court appoint a referee. The referee will review the facts and circumstances listed in the foreclosure action and render his or her report to the court. This report includes the amount due and owing, any facts relevant to the case, and a report of any additional costs involved, such as *board-ups*, that is, boarding up doors and windows and securing the property against vandals; legal fees; court costs; and so forth. The judge then issues a judgment of foreclosure and sale in favor of the foreclosing lender and directs the referee to sell the property at a certain date and time at a public auction.

The referee must advertise the auction sale according to the requirements of local statutes. After all the mandated legal procedures are completed, the auction is held. At the auction, the referee reads the terms of sale to the public and opens the bidding at the upset price stipulated by the courts.

A Trust Deed Foreclosure

Trust deeds are similar to mortgages except that the trust deed is a three-party instrument. The borrower is called the *trustor*, and the lender is the *beneficiary*. The third party is an intermediary, called the *trustee*. The trustee's job is to hold the title to the property on behalf of the beneficiary, as security for the payment of the debt. Due to the *power-of-sale clause* found in all trust deeds, if the trustor does not make the loan payments, the trustee can sell the property at a public auction without having to obtain permission from the courts. The trustee simply records a notice of default, sends a copy to the trustor, and after 90 days, a notice of sale is posted on the property. The sale is advertised to the public for the required period of time, and if payment is still not made by the trustor to cover the arrears, the property is auctioned. Lenders prefer trust deeds to mortgages because with trust deeds they can regain their property much faster since there is no need to first go through the courts to foreclose as there is with a mortgage.

Both the deed of trust and the mortgage serve the same purpose; the only major difference is the method of enforcement in a case where the borrower defaults. In any event, it is most important to remember that *lenders are not required by law to foreclose*. However, should they choose to do so, they must follow the procedure mandated by the laws of the state where the property is located.

The Soldier's and Sailor's Civil Relief Act of 1940

In some cases, a lender must modify a foreclosure action in order to comply with the Soldier's and Sailor's Civil Relief Act of 1940. Under this act, when property is owned by a person who is in active military duty and the mortgage loan was originated prior to the commencement of that military duty, then no sale, foreclosure, or seizure of property for nonpayment of any sum due will be valid if it is made during the period of the military service, or within several months thereafter. This does not apply if the courts think that the ability of the delinquent homeowner to comply with the terms of the loan obligation is not materially affected by reason of the homeowner's involvement in military service, or if the foreclosure sale was granted by the courts before the active duty began. Under the act, active-duty military personnel may be allowed a reduction of interest rates on debts, including mortgages, if their military service involvement impairs their ability to pay their loans at the current interest rates. Repayment plans and extensions of time to pay can also be worked out.

Consult a mortgage expert or attorney for more information about the specific foreclosure procedures that apply in your state.

Opportunities for Purchasing Foreclosures

Now let's explore the available opportunities for purchasing properties before, during, and after the foreclosure. In the chapters that follow, we will take an in-depth look at these opportunities in order to determine both the benefits and risks involved, as well as the procedures that must be followed. Along the way, you will learn some of the secrets which up to now were known only by successful professional investors.

2
The Basics of Buying Foreclosures At the Auction

A Day at an Auction

To begin a typical day at a foreclosure auction, let's review the overall procedure that is followed.

The Opening Bid Amount

First, there's an *opening bid amount*, also known as an *upset price*, which is the amount that begins the auction bidding. The opening bid amount usually includes the mortgage balance, interest and back taxes, court costs, legal fees, and the liens and judgments attached to the premises before the default and during the time the property was owned by the delinquent party. These debts are normally satisfied at the closing with the money paid by the successful high bidder.

The Bidding Procedure

When I attended my first foreclosure sale to obtain a property, I had visions of an auctioneer holding a huge gavel and yodeling out bid amounts from behind a podium. Instead, I was surprised to find that, after the referee announced that the sale was about to begin, verbal bidding was conducted in a quiet and organized manner — with no yodeling and no gavel!

Many people may attend an auction, but this doesn't mean that all the people are there to bid on a property. Many people go to auctions merely out of curiosity. Others go to familiarize themselves with the auction procedure before they bid, thereby eliminating the intimidation factor that's involved whenever we try something new.

On the other hand, you may find that you're the only one attending an auction. Should this happen, you will be able to buy the property at the opening bid amount offered by the referee because there will be no competitors to bid up the price.

Methods Used for Bidding on Foreclosures

When the auction begins, the referee will explain the bidding procedure to be followed, and he or she will identify the property or properties up for bid. By "identify," I mean that the referee gives a legal description of the property and any related tax map designations. Information such as distinctive architectural features that may make the property more attractive to a buyer is not necessarily given.

There may be different methods used to bid on foreclosures at auctions. Some auctions are conducted by *verbal bidding*, in which the bidder calls out the amount desired as his or her offer on the property to be purchased. Another method used for bidding at auctions involves *sealed written offers*. These offers are given to the designated authority who opens them and announces the successful high bidder's name and bid amount. Some auction procedures require you to register before bidding and show proof that you have the resources necessary for your down payment.

The High Bidder

If you, as high bidder, are awarded the contract for the premises in a bank auction situation, you must immediately render a required down payment (usually 10 percent of the bid amount) in the form of a money order, bank check, or certified funds, as required by the referee. (Later on, I will show you how to calculate the 10 percent you will need, as well as who to ask about the down payment information.) The referee will then issue the certificate of sale, which is the contract of sale that is executed and delivered to you as the successful high bidder.

Thirty Days to Close in Bank Auctions

You will be expected to "close" with the 90 percent balance due within a certain period of time—usually 30 days after the contract is signed. Under certain circumstances, you may be granted an extension (extra time to close). For example, if your attorney is on vacation, you may need to ask for an extension until he or she returns. Normally, however, if you're the successful high bidder at a bank auction, you will be expected to close by the end of the usual 30-day period stipulated in the contract. Auction authorities can be rather strict in their requirement that high bidders adhere to the 30-day closing period limit because it is a common practice for high bidders to attempt to stall the closing time so that they can use that extra time to find the necessary financing.

Unusual Closing Delays

I was once involved in an unusual circumstance in which the *referee* required an extension of more than a year because a necessary legal document was missing. Before I explain the details of this case at greater length, some background information on the nature of the document in question is in order.

In New York, as well as 21 other states, real property is conveyed either through a deed (see Figure 2-1) or a *Torrens title,* also known as an owner's duplicate certificate of title (ODC). Torrens titles originated many years ago in Australia as the method used to record real property transactions there. However, deeds and Torrens titles are *not* interchangeable documents. One cannot be replaced with the other.

An original Torrens title is manila-colored and has a gold seal on the front page. Also on the front page is a legal description of the property, just as in a deed. But, unlike a deed, the Torrens title contains a listing of the *memorials.* This listing includes all the legal instruments (mortgages, liens, judgments, and satisfactions) that have been recorded on the property from its origin. Figure 2-2 is an example of a Torrens title.

THIS INDENTURE, made the   day of   , nineteen hundred and

BETWEEN

party of the first part, and

party of the second part,

WITNESSETH, that the party of the first part, in consideration of Ten Dollars and other valuable consideration paid by the party of the second part, does hereby grant and release unto the party of the second part, the heirs or successors and assigns of the party of the second part forever,

ALL that certain plot, piece or parcel of land, with the buildings and improvements thereon erected, situate, lying and being in the

TOGETHER with all right, title and interest, if any, of the party of the first part in and to any streets and roads abutting the above described premises to the center lines thereof; TOGETHER with the appurtenances and all the estate and rights of the party of the first part in and to said premises; TO HAVE AND TO HOLD the premises herein granted unto the party of the second part, the heirs or successors and assigns of the party of the second part forever.

AND the party of the first part covenants that the party of the first part has not done or suffered anything whereby the said premises have been encumbered in any way whatever, except as aforesaid.
AND the party of the first part, in compliance with Section 13 of the Lien Law, covenants that the party of the first part will receive the consideration for this conveyance and will hold the right to receive such consideration as a trust fund to be applied first for the purpose of paying the cost of the improvement and will apply the same first to the payment of the cost of the improvement before using any part of the total of the same for any other purpose.
The word "party" shall be construed as if it read "parties" whenever the sense of this indenture so requires.

IN WITNESS WHEREOF, the party of the first part has duly executed this deed the day and year first above written.

IN PRESENCE OF:

FORMS MAY BE PURCHASED FROM JULIUS BLUMBERG, INC., NY, NY OR ANY OF ITS DEALERS. REPRODUCTION PROHIBITED.

Standard N.Y.B.T.U. Form 8002. Bargain and Sale Deed, with Covenant Against Grantor's Acts—Individual or Corporation.

Figure 2-1. A standard deed.

THE LAND TITLE REGISTRATION LAW

Owner's Duplicate Certificate of Title

No. 99632	FIRST REGISTERED April 23. 1949
TRANSFER FROM	CERTIFICATE No. 92073

I, LESTER M. ALBERTSON, Registrar of the County of Suffolk, in the State of New York, DO HEREBY CERTIFY THAT

of

are the owners of an Estate

in the following Land: ALL that certain plot, piece or parcel of land, with the buildings and improvement thereon erected, situate, lying and being in the Town of Islip, County of Suffolk, State of New York, known and designated at a certain map entitled, "Map of Islip Park Estates developed by Frederick Farms Inc., 258 Broadway, N.Y.C., surveyed by George H. Walbridge C.E. and Surveyor, Babylon, N.Y." and filed in the Suffolk County Clerk's Office on Map No. 1717 on November 25, 1949 as all by Lot No. 96 being bounded and described as follows BEGINNING at a point on the easterly side of Bay Shore Avenue at a point distant 200.00 feet northerly as measured along the easterly side of Bay Shore Avenue from the corner formed by the intersection of its intersection with the northerly side of Belmont Street; running thence north 0 degree 02 minutes 10 seconds west along the easterly side of Bay Shore Avenue 60 feet; thence north 89 degrees 57 minutes 50 seconds east 178.00 feet; thence south 0 degrees 02 minutes 10 seconds east 60 feet; thence south 89 degrees 57 minutes 50 seconds west 178.00 feet to the easterly side of Bay Shore Avenue at the point or place of BEGINNING.

SUBJECT to the estates, easements, encumbrances and charges hereunder noted.

WITNESS my hand and official seal at

Riverhead, N.Y., this 19th day November, 1975.

Registrar

Figure 2-2. A Torrens title.

The deed or Torrens title, depending on which of the two is used, will be among the important documents sent to new homeowners by their attorney after all required documents have been recorded.

If a homeowner loses a deed after it has been recorded, it can be replaced for a few dollars simply by requesting a duplicate copy from the office of the county clerk in the county where the property is located. If a homeowner loses a Torrens title, however, a *court order* is required in many states to replace it with another original Torrens title. This procedure can take many months, and in one foreclosure purchase in which I was involved, it took well over a year! *In states where the Torrens system has not been simplified, property under a Torrens title can never be conveyed without the original document. A copy can never be used.*

Because the original Torrens title is most likely in the possession of the delinquent homeowner who is about to be foreclosed on, it is oftentimes difficult for the foreclosing lender or its representative to obtain the title. The delinquent borrower is unlikely to cooperate with the foreclosing lender by making the document available because this would expedite the sale of the borrower's home to someone else. The foreclosing lender must now go through the courts to get a replacement Torrens title in order to be able to convey the property to the successful high bidder.

Many people who are purchasing foreclosures need all the time they can get between the time the contract is drawn up and the actual closing in order to obtain the appropriate financing. Therefore, they would benefit greatly from any extra time it would take the lender to obtain a court order for a new Torrens title to be issued. I wonder how many foreclosure purchasers specifically bid on properties under a Torrens title with this very purpose consciously in mind. At any rate, it's easy to see why it would be in the purchaser's best interests to do so, and to find out at the earliest opportunity whether a particular property will be conveyed using a regular deed or by a Torrens title. This information can be found in the foreclosure search and report that the foreclosing lender ordered when the foreclosure action began.

With all this in mind, we can return now to the case in which I was personally involved. The foreclosing lender was unable to get the original Torrens title from the delinquent borrower. As a result, the investor for whom I was managing the property had to wait over a year as the successful high bidder before the referee was able to go through the courts to obtain a new original Torrens title. By the time the property closed, the investor had plenty of time to secure financing and work out a rental agreement with the occupants. This is not to imply that the procedure to obtain a new Torrens title will *always* take as long as it did in this and many similar cases, but simply to make you aware that the very strong possibility of its happening this way is clearly present. Your state may have legislation that makes it unnecessary for a lender without access to the original Torrens certificate to go through the courts for a new one. Contact your attorney or title expert for information about the Torrens system in your area of interest.

Warning: Peculiar Purchase Ahead

Foreclosure purchases are different from a normal purchase between a buyer and a seller. Let's look at the distinguishing characteristics of buying a foreclosure as compared to a typical conventional purchase.

Buying for Less Than Market Value

Normally, you pay close to market value, or maybe a little less, for a typical property purchase. For a foreclosure purchased at an auction, however, you can pay a *small fraction* of the price you would pay in a typical purchase because the purchase price is based on the *mortgage balance* and *not* on the market value.

An investor I know purchased a property at an auction in Westhampton Beach on Long Island, New York, that was worth approximately $1 million for $167,000. He was the only bidder at the auction and won by bidding one dollar over the upset price. The auction happened to take place on the day Hurricane Gloria hit. Many "seasoned" foreclosure purchasers will vow that the best time to bid on a property is during poor weather conditions, when fewer people will venture out to an auction!

No Down Payment Refunds

In a conventional purchase, there is usually a *mortgage contingency clause* in the contract whereby if you are unable to get a mortgage or some other method of bank financing, you are entitled to have your down payment refunded. However, for foreclosures purchased at an auction, it is possible for there to be *no* contingency clause allowing down payment refunds. This means that if you cannot come up with the cash required to complete the transaction within the stipulated 30-day period from the contract date, you could lose your down payment.

You will need to check with the referee, or have your attorney examine the contract, in order to confirm that the down payment itself would be considered as the total amount collected as "liquidated damages" and that the referee would not hold you responsible if, as the successful high bidder, you were unable to close and the property had to be reauctioned and subsequently sold for less money. Some contracts may contain wording that holds you responsible for the difference in your original bid amount and the lower reauctioned amount.

I once had a man come to one of my seminars on purchasing foreclosures who was going to attend his first auction on the following day. He planned to bring his entire life savings of $15,000 to use as a down payment in case he was the successful high bidder. He didn't realize that the contract would require a closing within 30 days, so he expected that the referee would wait for him to get a mortgage in order to close— even if it took several months. He literally turned pale and broke out into a cold sweat when he learned how close he had come to losing his entire life savings!

The Burden of Dispossessing Occupants

In a typical purchase, you can expect the premises to be "broom-clean" and vacant on the closing date, unless the property is bought subject to a lease and there is a tenant already residing in the property who is expected to remain there. When you buy a foreclosure, however, the burden of dispossessing any of the current occupants falls on you as the successful high bidder after the closing has taken place.

Buying in "As-Is" Condition

Another distinction between foreclosures and typical purchases involves representations about the property's condition. In a normal purchase, you expect the roof to be free of leaks, and the plumbing, heating, electrical systems, and appliances to be in good working order. Because foreclosure proceedings are indicative of a distressed situation, you cannot expect the same representations that the property is in good repair. Foreclosure purchases are sold in *as-is condition*. What you see, or don't see, is what you get—or don't get! People who are losing their homes are not likely to keep up with repairs or cosmetic appearance. You must remember that when buying a foreclosure, you are dealing with an "entity" (the lending institution) whose sole purpose is to sell at the highest price possible in order to recapture its losses. You are not dealing with a typical seller whose contract terms usually require that the property be sold in good condition.

The Delinquent Borrower's Right of Redemption

Another foreclosure idiosyncrasy is the *right of redemption* available to the previous delinquent homeowner. The right of redemption is available to everyone who owns real estate, and allows a delinquent homeowner to reclaim property by paying all of the debt (the upset price) up until the public bidding begins. Remember, once the default proceeding begins, the delinquent homeowners can no longer simply pay the outstanding monthly payments. They are now responsible for the *entire* mortgage balance, plus accumulated charges and legal fees.

In some states, delinquent homeowners' right of redemption may allow them to reclaim their property *even after* the auction by paying the upset price. In other states, the owner's right of redemption is over once the bidding begins and the delinquent homeowner can only reclaim the property if he or she is the successful high bidder. Sometimes there are exceptions regarding unpaid federal tax liens. Check with your local expert to confirm the redemption procedures that apply in your state.

3

The Basics
of Buying
Foreclosures
After the Auction

Defining Bank-owned Properties

Bank-owned properties are foreclosures that are available to be purchased *after* the auction. In order to understand the concept of buying bank-owned property, you'll need to understand how the property became a part of the lender's inventory. There are a number of reasons why a property becomes bank-owned.

No Bids Are Made at the Auction

Sometimes, nobody shows up to bid on a property offered at an auction. Perhaps the opening bid amount exceeds the public's perceived value of the property, and therefore, it's not considered a buy. For example, if you think the value of a property offered at an auction is only $100,000 and the liens, judgments, legal fees, and other costs bring the upset price up to $125,000, then this would obviously *not* be a property to bid on.

Another reason people may not show up at an auction is because of poor weather conditions. Some people lose their motivation to attend auctions during severe storms or other potentially dangerous climatic disturbances.

Lastly, people may not show up at an auction because it was rescheduled and the public was not aware of the new date.

Friendly Foreclosures

Sometimes a property is not auctioned because the delinquent homeowner has turned over the deed to the foreclosing lender and moved out of the property before a foreclosure action commenced. This procedure is called giving a *deed in lieu of foreclosure,* and is also known as a *friendly foreclosure.* In some states and in many situations, a lender will accept a deed in lieu of foreclosure from a delinquent borrower in order to bypass the expense of the foreclosure procedure. The delinquent borrower benefits by avoiding a foreclosure action (which will damage the delinquent borrower's credit rating) as well as the possibility of a *deficiency judgment* filed against the delinquent borrower. A deficiency judgment is a judgment that can be filed against the delinquent borrower after the foreclosure occurs if the auction or sale fails to produce enough money to cover the outstanding debts. For example, if the judgment amount of the foreclosure is $100,000 and the property subsequently sells for $80,000, there could be a $20,000 deficiency judgment for which the delinquent borrower is held responsible. This could result in garnished wages and tarnished credit ratings. Deficiency judgments do not apply in trust deed states.

Although giving up a deed in lieu of foreclosure eliminates the chance of a deficiency judgment, it is not always the most beneficial solution for everyone. Normally, when a lender forecloses on a delinquent borrower and the property goes to auction, if the property is "bid up," that is, if amounts are offered above the upset price, then the overage goes to the delinquent borrower, who may now use the extra money to satisfy additional outstanding debts. When a borrower gives the deed in lieu of foreclosure, he or she also forfeits the right to receive any overages that may result from a subsequent sale. For example, if the upset price is $100,000 and the property is bid up at the auction to $120,000, the delinquent borrower is entitled to the $20,000 difference and would get that money unless he or she has given up the deed in lieu of foreclosure. In areas where the market has not depreciated tremendously, there is a chance that an auction *will* bring in an overage above the upset price, and a delinquent homeowner who gives a deed in lieu of foreclosure could lose money.

A Lender's View of Bank-Owned Property

If a property is not sold at the auction, the lender "buys it back" and the property is now owned by the foreclosing lender and is taken back into the lender's inventory. In cases where the delinquent borrower has given the deed in lieu of foreclosure, the property is also taken into the lender's inventory. The property is now bank-owned, also known as an REO (real-estate-owned). Lenders designate different names for their bank-owned property. Some lenders simply call them bank-owned real estate.

Bank-owned property is a burden to a lending institution. Many lenders do not have the management capabilities to hold onto these properties for long periods of time. The lender has to bear the expenses of paying property and other taxes along with the costs of repairs and the threat of vandalism. These properties are ripe for purchase at outstanding savings because the lender is a truly motivated seller.

Finding REOs

Years ago, lending institutions would not admit that they had properties in their inventories that had been taken back from delinquent borrowers. It could hurt a lender's public image should potential borrowers think that the lending institution would take drastic action (such as foreclosing) if borrowers didn't pay their mortgages. Most lending institutions are trying to get the public to come to them for mortgage money to buy houses, and it would work against the lenders to broadcast the fact that they have foreclosed on people's homes in the past for nonpayment of loans.

However, because of today's troubled economy and the vast numbers of properties that lenders have had to take back, many lending institutions have "come out of the closet," as it were, and are willing to openly admit that they have bank-owned foreclosures available. Some lenders even prepare lists of their bank-owned properties that they offer to the public, along with attractive financing terms to make the properties easier to buy.

You can contact your local lenders and ask for their foreclosure department or their asset-recovery division (or whatever department is in charge of their bank-owned property). Ask them to send you a list of their available properties and the bidding procedures required for you to make an offer to purchase any property or properties that interest you. Many of these lists will include the addresses of the available properties, along with the asking prices, access, pictures of the properties, information about the property taxes, and lot sizes.

Not all lending institutions will have bank-owned foreclosures in their inventory. Some lenders have always been very strict with qualifying procedures for borrowers and their appraisal guidelines were always tight. This may mean that they have not given risky loans, and therefore, they have not yet had to foreclose on their borrowers.

Buying REOs

After you have contacted lending institutions and received their lists of available properties, inspect them and make an offer based on what is a good deal for you. Once a property becomes bank-owned, there's a greater flexibility in the offers that can be accepted, especially if the bank has a large number of them. Remember, these properties are doing nothing but sitting in the lender's inventory, costing the bank money and waiting to be vandalized. In this situation, you're dealing with lenders directly by mailing in your offer instead of the verbal bidding that occurs at an auction.

The offer you make for an REO should be as specific as possible. Here are the important items to include in your written offer:

The address.   Clearly indicate the address of the property you are offering to purchase. The lending institution that sent you the list may have designated an identification number to each of the properties they are offering. Be certain to clearly specify the exact address of the property you are submitting your offer on.

The purchase price.   Your offer should include the purchase price, that is, the amount of money you are offering to buy the property.

The deposit.   Some lending institutions may require you to send in a deposit (also called a *binder*) along with your offer. The deposit is usually a nominal amount ($100) that will be refunded to you if your offer is not accepted. If your offer is accepted, the deposit would be applied to (deducted from) the purchase price.

The financing terms.   If you want the lender to provide you with financing for the property you purchase from them, your offer should include the financing terms you would like the lender to set. These terms should include the interest rate you wish to pay, the amount you want to borrow, and the length of time of the mortgage (15, 20, or 30 years).

The down payment.   If the lending institution you are purchasing the property from is providing financing, the difference between the amount they will lend you, and the purchase price, is the down payment. For example, let's say you wish to purchase an REO from the lender and you offer $100,000 as your purchase price. You ask them to provide financing (mortgage money) in the amount of $85,000 at 10 percent for 30 years. You will need to come up with $15,000 as your down payment. Some lenders may require you to give the down payment when your offer is accepted and the contract is signed. Other lenders will require that you give the down payment later on, when you close on the property. The list of properties that the lender sends you may include the down payment requirements, or you can call the lender directly to ask what their requirements are.

The closing date.   Your offer should stipulate the day you wish to take ownership and possession.

Your contact information.   Be certain to have your name, address, and telephone number on the letter so that the lending institution can contact you with a decision regarding your offer.

See Figure 3-1 for a sample offer letter sent to a lending institution about a bank-owned property.

Buying an REO Versus Buying a Property at Auction

The differences between purchasing a foreclosure property at a bank auction and purchasing an REO (after the auction) can vary from property to property. One difference you may find is that most REOs have clear titles. The lending institution will usually satisfy the outstanding liens and judgments attached to the property when they take the property into their inventory. If you purchase a property at an auction, the property may or may not have other liens and judgments attached to it,

---

Today's Date

XYZ Bank
000 Smith Street
Anytown, USA
Attn: Foreclosure Department

Dear _____ :

With reference to the property located at _____ ,
_____ , I would like to submit the following offer:

Purchase price:
Down payment:
Financing terms:
Closing date:

Amount enclosed (deposit/binder):

Please contact me at your earliest convenience with your acceptance.

My telephone number is: (_____) _____ .
My current address is:

Very truly yours,

Figure 3-1. A sample offer letter for a bank-owned property.

and you would be responsible for them if any did exist. The status of
the title will be covered in greater detail in Chapter 10.

Another difference you will find concerns the purchase price of the
property. A lending institution will base the asking price of an REO on
market value or a little less. A property offered at a bank auction is usu-

ally set at a lower price because it is based on the mortgage balance plus the back taxes, court costs, and legal fees. Once a lending institution takes a property back into its inventory the asking price will be based on market value or a little less. For example, if a property is valued at $100,000 and the mortgage balance plus accumulated charges (including court costs, legal fees, and back taxes) totals $60,000, the opening bid amount would be $60,000. If the property is not sold at the auction for any reason, and the lender has to take it back into its inventory, the property will now be offered for its $100,000 value, or a little less. Although the asking price may be higher when it becomes bank-owned, many lenders are very flexible and will entertain all reasonable offers on their REOs.

Another distinction is that most lending institutions will have ousted (evicted) any occupants from the REO before you buy it. This would eliminate the expense of eviction procedures that you would probably incur if you purchased a property at an auction where you would be responsible for evicting any of the current occupants after you became the new owner.

One final difference is that many lenders will offer financing to people who purchase their bank-owned property. Remember, the property is a nonperforming "liability" that costs the lenders money each month, and it is beneficial for them to offer good financing terms to a buyer who will assume the responsibilities of ownership of the property and who will pay the monthly mortgage. When you purchase a property at a bank auction, on the other hand, you will need to pay for your purchase with *cash*, or find financing elsewhere.

4
The Basics of Buying Foreclosures Before the Auction

Direct Contact With
Delinquent Homeowners

Direct contact with delinquent homeowners is another way of obtaining foreclosures. You may be able to obtain property *before* the auction using this method with people who are about to be foreclosed on. Foreclosure purchasers like this technique because it can allow them to take over the property, and hopefully, the existing mortgage, with little or no cash outlay.

Finding Delinquent Homeowners

You can find people who are delinquent with their mortgage payments and who are facing foreclosure through several methods.

Legal notices in local newspapers. You can find homeowners who are facing foreclosure in the legal notices section of your local newspaper. It is a required part of the foreclosure procedure for public notice to be given prior to the auction and the legal notices will list the property address, the name of the delinquent borrower, and other required legal information.

***Lis pendens* lists.**   Another way to find delinquent borrowers is by examining *lis pendens* lists. (*Lis pendens* is Latin for *action pending*.) These are lists of pending action that a foreclosing lender's attorney files with the court as part of the foreclosure action. You can preview these lists at the county clerk's office in the county where the property is located. There are also companies that sell *lis pendens* lists. You can look up names of such companies in reference books in your local library. Look under *real estate* for these books, e.g., *Gayles Directory*, and for specific magazines. And sometimes the publishers of upcoming auction lists will offer *lis pendens* lists as an additional service in order to give subscribers a chance to buy property before *and* during the auction.

Seminars for delinquent homeowners.   You can attend seminars on avoiding foreclosure that are open to the public. Sometimes attorneys or accountants will conduct seminars in order to develop their client base. People who are about to lose their homes may attend these seminars, and you may be able to arrange to buy a property from them directly. If you feel tacky or uncomfortable about approaching people who are in such financial trouble, you might try some creative alternatives. One such alternative is to have a T-shirt designed with lettering on it that says, "I buy foreclosures. Quick closings." If you try this method, you can just sit at the seminar and wait for people to approach you. Another alternative is to distribute business cards with your name and telephone number where you can be contacted on them. The business cards can also be printed to include wording on them that identifies you as a foreclosure purchaser.

Get a real estate license.   Many people go into the real estate field and get their real estate salesperson's license in order to have access to opportunities for buying real estate at bargain prices. When homeowners are facing a severe financial problem and they need to sell their home quickly to avoid losing everything, they may go to a real estate office and offer to sell their $150,000 house for $100,000. And what would a real estate professional do in that situation? Buy it! Many of the people who are in my licensing school right now are getting licensed in order to have access to great deals like this.

The Benefits of Buying Before the Auction

The ideal scenario for buying before the auction is to find a homeowner who has not paid the mortgage for a few months and who is therefore about to be foreclosed on. The homeowner must be willing to move out and sell you the house. You will agree to assume the mortgage and perhaps give the homeowner a certain amount of money in order to help him or her out of the financial hole into which they've fallen. The homeowner can now move away and begin a new life without the huge burden and stress of financial problems to handle.

Let's explore a situation in which you have found just such a homeowner. You see a property listed in the legal notices of your newspaper and you contact the delinquent homeowner. You arrange a meeting and find out that the mortgage balance is $90,000 and that three mortgage payments have been missed. The homeowner is unable to catch up with the delinquent payments, has lost his job, and wants to move to a different state with a lower cost of living. You have valued the property at $125,000 and the homeowner has agreed to sell you the property for $95,000 if you give him $5000 in cash and assume his $90,000 loan responsibility. You and the delinquent homeowner approach the lender who is about to foreclose on the property. The lender has not gotten a mortgage payment for 3 months and knows that the homeowner is unable to catch up and repay the arrears. The lender now has to begin the distasteful and expensive procedure of foreclosing on the delinquent borrower. Here you come, the proverbial knight in shining armor, and offer to take over the delinquent homeowner's mortgage payments *and* save the lender from this unsavory situation.

Depending on the market conditions in the area, and the number of potential and active foreclosures the lender is currently dealing with, the lender may agree to let you take over the mortgage, and may even "forgive," or waive, the back-payment arrears as well. If the mortgage is not supposed to be assumable, or if the original homeowner had gotten the mortgage for a very low interest rate (and the rates are now substantially higher), the lender may want to renegotiate the rate with you, but will still give you favorable terms. For example, if the previous homeowner had a 7 percent fixed interest rate and the prevailing rate is now 10 percent, the lender may agree to let you assume the mortgage for a renegotiated amount of between 8 and 9 percent. This interest rate is better than the original rate for the lender, and it is also beneficial for you because it is a below-market rate. In this scenario, you have obtained a $125,000 property for $95,000. Your total cash outlay is $5000 with little or no closing costs. Situations will always vary; the lender may not waive the back payments, or may not let you assume a mortgage that was unassumable, but this example was used to illustrate the concept and the benefits of purchasing foreclosures before the auction.

Understanding the Delinquent Owner

Before you start to knock on the doors of people who are going to be foreclosed on, it's important for you to understand the psychological effect that pending foreclosure must be having on them, as well as the other alternatives that are available to them. When you approach them to try to buy their homes, they may welcome you and invite you in for coffee – or they may slam the door in your face!

As a purchaser of foreclosures for myself and for other investors, I have spoken to a lot of people to find out what had happened to cause them to fall so far behind. The most common reasons I have heard include illnesses or accidents that had put the owner in arrears. Some were laid off or fired from their jobs. In many cases, divorce had taken its toll. Some people had taken an equity loan to start a business that failed, and that extra monetary obligation was choking them. But the most prevalent cause was ignorance. *They just didn't believe it could happen to them.* They "put their heads in the sand" and figured that somehow, somewhere, someone would bail them out before they lost their homes.

Overcoming the Delinquent Owner's Objections

In the real estate business, we learn to overcome objections in order to be successful in closing our deals. Here are some of the reasons or methods that the delinquent homeowners will use to avoid dealing with you when you offer to purchase the property from them.

They are selling the house.   The delinquent homeowners may say that they are going to try to put the house on the market for a lot more money than you are offering. Many times the people who are facing foreclosure *will* try to sell the house, but have it listed too high, even though they risk losing everything if they can't sell it in time to keep it from going to auction. Some foreclosing lenders will delay the auction if the delinquent homeowner can prove that the property is in contract with a bona fide purchaser. This is the advantage you can offer the homeowner as an incentive for dealing with you. If they are not responsive or they resist your attempt to discuss your purchase terms, just give them your business card, or write your name and contact number on a piece of paper for them. Keep in touch with them weekly to see how successful they are with their attempts to sell the house. If they are un-successful, they may start to get scared and may be more receptive to your offer, especially if you are offering terms that include a quick clos-ing date.

They are filing for bankruptcy.   Another way people save their homes from foreclosure is by filing for bankruptcy. If homeowners choose to file for bankruptcy in order to save their home, they are not excused from paying their monthly mortgage payments. Also, some forms of bankruptcy require a reorganization plan for debt consolidation and may be turned down by the courts because the people don't have enough steady income to repay their debts. Give them your business card and keep in touch with them. If their bankruptcy plans fall through, they may decide to sell the property to you after all.

They are getting a hard-money loan.   Some delinquent homeowners get a *hard-money loan* and they intend to use the money they borrow to bring their delinquent mortgage current. A hard-money loan is differ-ent from "break-your-arm" financing by a loan shark. This type of loan includes high interest rates and high points, but the loan approval is based on the equity in the home and not on a good credit rating. Many times the fees that are charged are so exorbitant that they will eat up the entire equity available. This could mean that the delinquent homeowner would not have enough money from the loan to pay off all the arrears. Again, give them your business card and keep in touch with them. If they're unable to get the loan, they may decide to sell the prop-erty to you.

They are working out a payment plan.   Another alternative available to the delinquent homeowner is to work out a payment plan with the fore-closing lender. Sometimes payment plans are already in default and the lender may not be willing to work with the homeowners any longer. If they are unable to work with the foreclosing lender, they may decide to sell the property to you.

They will give the deed in lieu of foreclosure and leave.   As discussed earlier, in some cases the homeowners have the option of asking the lender to accept the deed in lieu of foreclosure. Again, if this alternative is used, the homeowners turn over the deed to the foreclosing lender and walk away from the property to avoid the foreclosure action, the damage to their credit rating, and the possibility of a deficiency judg-ment. This may not be the best alternative for the homeowner, and may not be allowed in trust deed states. The homeowner may be better off selling the property to you quickly, especially if you have an agreement that involves giving them additional cash with which to start over, and assuming their loan, thereby relieving them of the financial burden of a delinquent mortgage.

Win With Pleasant Persistence

When contacting delinquent homeowners, you need to be aware that they may still be in a state of denial and may not even be willing to speak to you. When this happens, patient, compassionate persistence will be your key to success. It has been my experience that in most cases the typical delinquent homeowner will not show interest in your offer to buy the property from them until the *fourth* time you approach them.

Dress for Success

If you are planning to meet with the delinquent homeowners face-to-face, you need to remember that you are dealing with people who are in financial trouble. Do you put on your best jewelry, wear your expensive designer suit, and have your airline ticket for a vacation to Hawaii sticking out of your pocket? *Of course not!* If these people are losing everything, they may resent anyone who isn't in the same situation and they may not want to deal with you. They may also try to negotiate a higher purchase price from you because you look as if you can well afford it. The best strategy in this case is to keep a low profile. Wear jeans or other casual clothing that is not intimidating. Your object is to create a comfortable atmosphere with a friendly attitude and a low-key appearance.

Letters That Open Doors

If you feel uncomfortable about approaching the delinquent homeowners on a face-to-face basis initially, you can send them a letter first. The letter can be typed or handwritten. A handwritten envelope is very important; it looks more personal. If the delinquent homeowners think you are trying to sell them something because your typed envelope looks too professional, they may automatically throw your letter away without even opening it. Also, it's important to use the homeowner's names for a more personal impression. The letter should indicate that you understand their problem, that everyone is in the same boat, and that they have nothing to be ashamed of. Keep the letter short, simple, and nonthreatening.

Figure 4-1 is a sample letter to a delinquent homeowner.

If you are fortunate enough to contact a delinquent homeowner who is open to negotiating with you, it is essential, especially if you are planning to assume the existing mortgage, that you make certain that, in addition to the agreed purchase price, there are no extra liens or judgments that you were unaware of, and which you would be responsible for. Your attorney should make sure that your contract with the delinquent homeowner is contingent upon the results of a title (or foreclosure) search, and should assist you in this area as

---

Today's Date

Delinquent Homeowner's Name
000 Smith Street
Anytown, USA

Dear _____ ,

I understand that you are having difficulty making your mortgage payments, as are many people in today's economy.

If you would be interested in talking to me about a quick sale, please call me at (_____) _____ .

Very truly yours,

(Your Name) _____

Figure 4-1. A sample letter to a delinquent homeowner.

well. Other contract terms should also include the repairs, if any, that the delinquent homeowner will complete prior to closing and the appliances, window treatments, and other furnishings or fixtures, e.g., air conditioners and carpeting, that will stay with the house as part of the purchase price.

5

Other Sources for Finding Foreclosures

Foreclosure Auction List
Publications

There are publishers of upcoming real estate foreclosure auction lists. These publications may be newspapers, magazines, newsletters, or simply a list of upcoming auctions. They are available to subscribers who wish to purchase them. These lists usually contain the following information about the upcoming foreclosure auction:

Property addresses

Time, place, and date of the auction

Upset price

Name of the foreclosing lender

Lender's attorney information

Referee information

Index number of the action

When choosing a particular publisher, you need to ask the following questions to determine who offers the best services to their subscribers, for the best price. I suggest the following questions:

What information do they give in their publication? Some publications give you the mortgage balance, the number of rooms in the property, the appraised value, the lot size, and in some states, information on whether the property is under a deed or a Torrens title. Obviously, the more information supplied to you as a subscriber, the better. Compare the information given to you by each publisher in order to choose the best publication for you.

What areas do they cover? If you are interested in properties located in more than one county or township, you would need to know whether all the areas you are interested in are included in the publication. On the other hand, if you are only interested in one specific county or township, you may not need a publication that covers a larger area.

How often does the publication come out? Foreclosure auction lists come out weekly, biweekly, and even monthly. My preference is for lists that come out weekly because this enables you to be up to date with the latest properties available.

Do the publishers offer support services and advice if you are a subscriber? This can be extremely valuable for inexperienced foreclosure purchasers, and might make the difference in your choice of one publication over another.

What is the publisher's fee, and do they offer discounted rates if you subscribe for longer periods? Some publishers will charge you a lower price if you subscribe to their publication for a longer term (that is, for 6 months rather than 3 months, or for 1 year rather than 6 months, and so forth). Also, you would want to know whether the fee is discounted if you subscribe to more than one county or township.

To find publishers of upcoming foreclosure auctions, you can look in the real estate section of your local newspaper. Some publishers advertise their auction lists under headings that attract investors, and some local newspapers have a special section strictly for foreclosure enthusiasts. You can contact your local newspaper and ask if there is a section where foreclosure list publishers advertise available lists. Another source might be your Yellow Pages under the heading, "Foreclosure Publications," or you may find foreclosure lists in a magazine form at your local newsstand.

Announcements in Local Newspapers

A foreclosing lender is required to publicize the fact that there is going to be an auction for a property. You can find information about upcoming auctions in the legal notices section of your local newspaper. The legal notice will give the name of the foreclosing lender, along with the name of the party the foreclosure action will be held against. The legal notice lists the index number of the action as well as the legal description of the property and other information required by the laws of the state.

Figure 5-1 is a sample legal notice.

Bankruptcy Sales

Bankruptcy sales are another source you can use to purchase foreclosures. Bankruptcy sales occur when an individual or a company needs to liquidate assets to pay off debtors. You can contact bankruptcy courts and ask to be put on their mailing list for real property sales. In bankruptcy sales, a court-appointed trustee accepts verbal or written bids by the public as noted in their publication. In some areas, you can go to the bankruptcy courts and examine their dockets. Be sure to call first because some bankruptcy courts may limit the dates and times you can get access to the dockets. For the telephone numbers of bankruptcy courts

L-8704
SUPREME COURT—COUNTY OF

SAVINGS BANK OF
Plaintiff against KE
et al
Defendant(s).
Pursuant to judgment of foreclosure and sale entered herein and dated December 28, 1990. I, the undersigned Referee will sell at public auction at the front steps of the tington Town Hall, 100 Main Street, on the 15th day of 1991 at 10:00 AM premises beginning at a point on the westerly side of 233.85 feet southerly from the southerly end of a curve connecting the westerly side of Katay Drive South (West Katay Street) with the southerly side of Effron Avenue, being a plot 100 feet by 200 feet, said premises known as 114 Drive, Town of

Approximate amount of lien $147,466.87 plus interest and costs. Premises will be sold subject to provisions of filed judgement. Index Number 2918/90. Dated February 11, 1991. Refᵒrᵉᵉ

Figure 5-1. A sample legal notice in a newspaper.

in your area, look under the heading of "Bankruptcy Courts" in your Yellow Pages.

Government Sales

Government sales occur when the United States government offers real estate and vacant land to the general public in order to increase tax revenues. This program is offered through the General Services Administration (GSA). You can write them and ask for their booklet. The booklet will give you the procedure to follow for ordering their "U.S. Real Property Sales List." The General Services Administration does not maintain a mailing list, so you will need to send in the order blank from each issue in order to get the next issue mailed to you. You can order lists of properties by state or for all 50 states, and you can select agricultural, commercial, industrial, and/or residential property lists. The General Services Administration accepts verbal and written bids as noted in their publication.

For issues of the "U.S. Real Property Sales List" catalog, write to:

Properties
E. Consumer Information Center
Pueblo, CO 81009
(617) 565-5700

For information about a specific state, refer to the following list of GSA regional offices.

GSA regional offices	States covered by regional office	
Boston Real Estate Office	Connecticut	New Jersey
U.S. General Services Administration	Illinois	New York
10 Causeway Street	Indiana	Ohio
Boston, MA 02222	Maine	Puerto Rico
(617) 565-5700	Massachusetts	Rhode Island
	Michigan	Vermont
	Minnesota	Virgin Islands
	New Hampshire	Wisconsin
Atlanta Sales Office	Alabama	Mississippi
U.S. General Services Administration	Delaware	North Carolina
75 Spring St., Rm. 818	District of Columbia	Pennsylvania
Atlanta, GA 30303	Florida	South Carolina
(404) 331-5133	Georgia	Tennessee
	Kentucky	Virginia
	Maryland	West Virginia

GSA regional offices	States covered by regional office	
Fort Worth Sales Office U.S. General Services Administration 819 Taylor St., Rm. 11A26 Fort Worth, TX 76102	Arkansas Colorado Iowa Kansas Louisiana Missouri Montana Nebraska	New Mexico North Dakota Oklahoma South Dakota Texas Utah Wyoming
San Francisco Sales Office U.S. General Services Administration 525 Market Street San Francisco, CA 94105 (415) 744-5952	Alaska Arizona California Guam Hawaii Idaho	Nevada Oregon Washington

Field offices
Office of Real Estate Sales   U.S. General Services Administration   230 South Dearborn St., Rm. 3756   Chicago, IL 60604   (312) 353-6045
Office of Real Estate Sales   U.S. General Services Administration   GSA Center, Rm. 2476   Auburn, WA 98001   (206) 931-7554

HUD Sales, or FHA Foreclosures

The U.S. Department of Housing and Urban Development (HUD) sales, also known as Federal Housing Administration (FHA) foreclosures, occur when a borrower defaults and the lender forecloses on an FHA loan. HUD pays the lending institution for the outstanding loan and expenses incurred. HUD takes ownership and resells the property to the public.

HUD requires that you go through their designated real estate brokers in order to inspect and bid on the foreclosures they're offering.

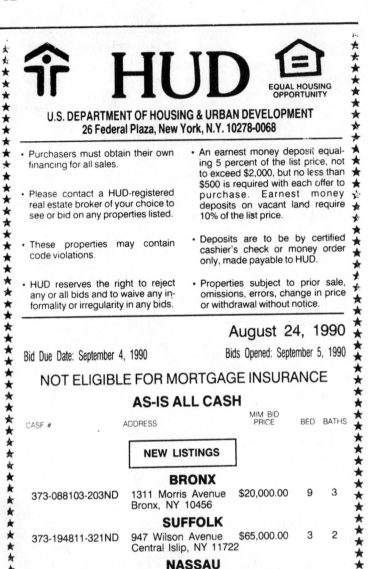

Figure 5-2. An illustration of a HUD advertisement.

HUD will give you a list of designated brokers to contact in your area of interest. The HUD area broker will prepare your bid and submit it to HUD for you. Sealed bids are accepted by mail, and you must include a 10 percent down payment with the bid. HUD will pay the real estate broker's fees if your offer is accepted.

In many cases, HUD will provide lower interest mortgages on these properties, but requires that you live in the house and not rent it out to others for a specified period (usually 3 years).

To find out about upcoming HUD/FHA sales and the designated HUD brokers in your area, contact your local HUD office. Many times, HUD will post upcoming auction information in local newspapers on a weekly basis. Figure 5-2 is an illustration of a HUD advertisement.

Veterans Administration (VA) Sales

Veterans Administration sales occur when the VA repossesses property from a serviceman or servicewoman who has been foreclosed on. You are *not* required to be a serviceperson or even an *owner-occupant* (someone who will buy the property to live in and not use it as a rental property) to purchase these properties. In some states you can purchase directly from the VA without using a real estate broker. VA "repos" usually require a 10 percent down payment with your bid, and those paying in cash are given first preference over someone who requires financing. Successful high bidders must satisfy steady employment and good credit criteria. Bidding is made through written offer.

The Veterans Administration's list of foreclosures is available on the first business day of each month. If you are a licensed real estate broker, the Veterans Administration in some states will allow you to send a copy of your real estate license in order to get a new list sent to you automatically each month. Otherwise, you must call each month to request a new list.

The names, addresses, and telephone numbers of Veterans Administration offices in each state are as follows:

Alabama

Veterans Administration Regional Office
474 South Court Street
Montgomery, AL 36104
(205) 832-7083

Alaska

Veterans Administration Regional Office
235 East 8th Avenue
Anchorage, AK 99501
(907) 271-4562

Arizona

Veterans Administration Regional
Office
3225 North Central Avenue
Phoenix, AZ 85012
(602) 241-2754

Arkansas

Veterans Administration Regional
Office
1200 West 3rd Street
Little Rock, AR 72201
(501) 378-5420

California

Veterans Administration Regional
Office
Federal Building
11000 Wilshire Blvd.
Los Angeles, CA 90024
(213) 209-7594

Veterans Administration Regional
Office
211 Main Street
San Francisco, CA 94105
(415) 974-0241

Colorado

Veterans Administration Regional
Office
Denver Federal Center
Building 20
Denver, CO 80225
(303) 980-2875

Connecticut

Veterans Administration Regional
Office
450 Main Street
Hartford, CT 06103
(203) 244-3537

Delaware

Veterans Administration Medical
and Regional Office Center

1601 Kirkwood Highway
Wilmington, DE 19805
(215) 951-5504

District of Columbia

Veterans Administration Regional
Office
941 North Capital Street, NE
Washington, DC 20421
(202) 275-1336

Florida

Veterans Administration Regional
Office
P.O. Box 1437
144 First Avenue, South
St. Petersburg, FL 33731
(813) 893-3433

Georgia

Veterans Administration Regional
Office
730 Peachtree Street, NE
Atlanta, GA 30365
(404) 347-3339

Hawaii

Veterans Administration Regional
Office
P.O. Box 50188, 96850
PJKK Federal Building
300 Ala Moana Blvd.
Honolulu, HI 96813
(808) 546-2160

Idaho

Veterans Administration Regional
Office
Federal Building and U.S.
Courthouse
550 West Fort Street
Box 044
Boise, ID 83724
(208) 334-1901

55

Illinois

Veterans Administration Regional Office
536 South Clark Street
P.O. Box 8136
Chicago, IL 60680
(312) 353-4056

Indiana

Veterans Administration Regional Office
575 North Pennsylvania Street
Indianapolis, IN 46204
(317) 269-7814

Iowa

Veterans Administration Regional Office
210 Walnut Street
Des Moines, IA 50309
(515) 284-4590

Kansas

Veterans Administration Medical and Regional Office Center
901 George Washington Blvd.
Wichita, KS 67211
(316) 269-6311

Kentucky

Veterans Administration Regional Office
600 Federal Place
Louisville, KY 40202
(502) 582-5861

Louisiana

Veterans Administration Regional Office
701 Loyola Avenue
New Orleans, LA 70113
(504) 589-6428

Maine

Veterans Administration Medical and Regional Office Center

Togus, ME 04330
(207) 623-8411

Maryland

Veterans Administration Regional Office
Federal Building
31 Hopkins Plaza
Baltimore, MD 21201
(301) 962-4467

Note. Montgomery and Prince Georges counties are under the jurisdiction of the Washington, DC Regional Office.

Massachusetts

Veterans Administration Regional Office
John F. Kennedy Building
Government Center
Boston, MA 02203
(617) 223-3053

Michigan

Veterans Administration Regional Office
Federal Building
477 Michigan Avenue
Detroit, MI 48226
(313) 226-4216

Minnesota

Veterans Administration Regional Office
Federal Building
Fort Snelling
St. Paul, MN 55111
(612) 725-4030

Mississippi

Veterans Administration Regional Office
100 West Capital Street
Jackson, MS 39269
(601) 960-4835

Missouri

Veterans Administration Regional
Office
Federal Building, Rm. 4705
1520 Market Street
St. Louis, MO 63103
(314) 425-5157

Montana

Veterans Administration Regional
Office
Fort Harrison, MT 59636
(406) 442-6410

Nebraska

Veterans Administration Regional
Office
Federal Building
100 Centennial Mall North
Lincoln, NE 68308
(402) 471-5031

Nevada

Veterans Administration Regional
Office
245 East Liberty Street
Reno, NV 89520

Note. Clark and Lincoln counties
are under the Los Angeles
Regional Office. Other counties are
consolidated with the San Francisco
Regional Office.

New Hampshire

Veterans Administration Regional
Office
Norris Cotton Federal Building
275 Chestnut Street
Manchester, NH 03101
(603) 666-7654

New Jersey

Veterans Administration Regional
Office

20 Washington Place
Newark, NJ 07102
(201) 645-3404

New Mexico

Veterans Administration Regional
Office
Dennis Chavez Federal Building
U.S. Courthouse
500 Gold Ave., SW
Albuquerque, NM 87102
(505) 766-2214

New York

Veterans Administration Regional
Office
Federal Building
111 West Huron Street
Buffalo, NY 14202
(716) 846-5292

Veterans Administration Regional
Office
252 Seventh Avenue
New York, NY 10001
(212) 620-6901

North Carolina

Veterans Administration Regional
Office
Federal Building
251 North Main Street
Winston-Salem, NC 27155
(919) 761-3498

North Dakota

Veterans Administration Regional
Office
655 First Avenue North
Fargo, ND 58102
(612) 725-4030

Note. Loan guarantee
consolidated with St. Paul,
Minnesota, Regional Office.

Ohio

Veterans Administration Regional
Office
Anthony J. Celebreeze Federal
Building
1240 East Ninth Street
Cleveland, OH 44199
(216) 522-3610

Oklahoma

Veterans Administration Regional
Office
125 South Main Street
Muskogee, OK 74401
(918) 687-2469

Oregon

Veterans Administration Regional
Office
Federal Building
1220 Southwest 3rd Avenue
Portland, OR 97204
(503) 221-2481

Pennsylvania

Veterans Administration Regional
Office
P.O. Box 8079
5000 Wissahickon Avenue
Philadelphia, PA 19101
(215) 951-5504

Veterans Administration Regional
Office
1000 Liberty Avenue
Pittsburgh, PA 15222
(412) 644-6657

Puerto Rico

Veterans Administration Regional
Office
GPO Box 4867
San Juan, PR 00936
(809) 753-4120

Rhode Island

Veterans Administration Regional
Office
380 Westminster Mall
Providence, RI 02903
(617) 223-3053
Note. Loan guarantee
consolidated with Boston Regional
Office.

South Carolina

Veterans Administration Regional
Office
1801 Assembly Street
Columbia, SC 29201
(803) 765-5841

South Dakota

Veterans Administration Regional
Office
P.O. Box 5046
2501 West 22nd Street
Sioux Falls, SD 57117
(612) 725-4030
Note. Loan guarantee
consolidated with St. Paul,
Minnesota, Regional Office.

Tennessee

Veterans Administration Regional
Office
110 Ninth Avenue, South
Nashville, TN 37203
(615) 251-5186

Texas

Veterans Administration Regional
Office
2515 Murworth Drive
Houston, TX 77054
(713) 660-4156

Veterans Administration Regional
Office
1400 North Valley Mills Drive
Waco, TX 76799

Utah

Veterans Administration Regional
Office
P.O. Box 11500
125 South State Street
Salt Lake City, UT 84147
(801) 588-5986

Vermont

Veterans Administration Medical
and Regional Office Center
White River Junction, VT 05001

Virginia

Veterans Administration Regional
Office
210 Franklin Road, SW
Roanoke, VA 24011
(703) 982-6135

Note. Arlington, Fairfax,
Loudoun, Prince William,
Spotsylvania, and Stafford counties
and the cities of Alexandria,
Fairfax, Falls Church, and
Fredricksburg are under the
jurisdiction of the Veterans
Administration Regional Office in
Washington, DC.

Washington

Veterans Administration Regional
Office
915 Second Avenue
Seattle, WA 98174
(206) 442-4096

West Virginia

Veterans Administration Regional
Office
640 4th Avenue
Huntington, WV 25701
(304) 529-5047

Note. Brooke, Hancock, Marshall,
and Ohio counties are under the
jurisdiction of the Veterans
Administration Regional Office in
Pittsburgh, PA.

Wisconsin

Veterans Administration Regional
Office
VA Center
P.O. Box 6
Wood, WI 53193
(414) 671-8174

Wyoming

Veterans Administration Medical
and Regional Office Center
2360 East Pershing Blvd.
Cheyenne, WY 82001
Note. Loan guarantee
consolidated with Denver Regional
Office.

6

How to Benefit From the Savings and Loan Disaster: Buying From the Resolution Trust Corporation

The Resolution Trust Corporation (RTC) is a large holder of foreclosed properties in the United States. It was created on August 9, 1989, when federal legislation instituted the Financial Institutions Reform, Recovery, and Enforcement Act (FIRREA) of 1989. The Resolution Trust Corporation is charged with selling troubled assets that the United States government has acquired from failed savings and loan associations.

The purpose of this chapter is to give the reader a basic understanding of the overall concept of the goals and workings of the Resolution Trust Corporation, as well as of related achievements involved in the development of this huge government wonder. It must be remembered that the RTC will alter its policies and procedures on an as-needed basis to serve the public's needs efficiently and effectively.

How the RTC Obtains Property

When a savings and loan association fails, the federal government, under prescribed rules and regulations, steps in and pays off all depositors with accounts of less than $100,000. The RTC must dispose of the assets held by the seized savings and loans in order to try to recover as much of the government's deposit insurance payouts as possible.

Financially troubled banks or savings and loans are put into *conservatorship*, which means that the institution still functions on a daily basis but a managing agent from the RTC is put in charge to try to rectify matters. If this proves to be impossible and the savings and loan becomes effectively dead, then it goes into *receivership*, which means that it is totally taken over by the RTC and its assets are liquidated.

The RTC's aim is to organize hundreds of billions of dollars worth of residential, commercial, and industrial properties so that the public can buy these properties as easily from the government as they can from a local real estate office. There will be a constant influx of new properties available as the federal government takes over additional savings and loans and clears the titles on foreclosed inventories.

Why the Cookie Crumbled

The general consensus regarding why many savings and loan associations have gotten into trouble includes a combination of many related and unrelated factors. Among these factors are depreciating real estate values, deregulation of the savings and loan industry, a failing economy, overbuilding, incompetent appraisal practices where values were inflated for mortgage purposes, and overzealous lenders who gave loans to borrowers who were not properly qualified. Recent federal legislation now demands unified standards for licensing and certifying appraisers, and lenders have tightened their qualifying guidelines for borrowers.

Getting Access to RTC Inventory Information

The RTC has provided access to most of its inventory of real estate assets that they have acquired from failed savings and loans. The inventory lists can be ordered in a variety of formats. These formats are designed to improve the public's access to the RTC's property listings.

Printed-Volume Format

There are printed inventory lists available in volumes, which you can order either separately or as a set. There is one volume for commercial property, another volume for industrial property, and two other volumes for residential property (one with listings of single-family properties and one with listings of multifamily properties, including condominiums and co-ops). The printed volumes are updated every 6 months. To order lists in the printed-volume format, call (800) 431-0600.

These volumes can also be found in many libraries throughout the United States. You can call the RTC directly for information about the location of libraries that have the printed volumes. The number to call for locations of libraries with RTC property lists is (800) 782-2990.

Personalized Printed Reports

Personalized printed reports on specific geographic areas can be ordered through the RTC and the reports will be delivered to you through the mail. The number to call for such lists is (800) RTC-3006.

5 1/4-inch Floppy Disks

Inventory lists can be obtained on 5-1/4-inch high-density floppy disks or nine-track tapes. You can order the entire list or you can order lists of properties individually by property type or by region by calling (703) 487-4068. The lists are updated monthly.

RTCNet On-line Computer System

These lists are also available to the public in an on-line computer system called RTCNet. It can be used by anyone with an IBM-compatible or Macintosh computer and a modem. You can order these lists by property type, list price, city, state, or Zip code. The information is available in either print- or download-form and is updated monthly. Subscribers to this service pay a subscription fee, a monthly user's fee, and a connection fee. These fees may be charged to a subscriber's credit card. Call (800) RTC-2990 to inquire about this service.

CD-ROM Disks

The RTC offers CD-ROM disks. This format allows RTC's inventory lists to be copied onto a computer's hard drive. You can order property information by geographic area, price, Zip code, county, or state. These lists are updated monthly. Call (800) RTC-2990 for information about this service.

For information regarding list updates for any of these services, call (800) 431-0600.

How the RTC Prices Its Properties

The RTC has been charged with establishing an appraisal or other valuation method for determining the market value of real property under the FIRREA Act of 1989. The FIRREA Act also stipulates that any real estate transaction that involves a property with a value greater than $15,000 (including the sale, lease, or purchase of real property or the use of real property as security for a loan or investment) requires an appraisal that is performed in accordance with RTC's standards.

Consequently, the RTC has established guidelines for determining the value of its properties and uses independent appraisal contractors to get information that ensures accurate pricing. It is the RTC's intent to sell these properties at market value. The RTC's market value may prove to be lower than the price an appraiser would set. Current policy allows the RTC to reduce a property's price by 10 percent after it remains on the market for 6 months (4 months for residential property). After another 3 months have passed, if the property still hasn't sold, then the price may be trimmed by another 5 percent. This means that the RTC can lower the market value by as much as 15 percent. This policy is subject to change. Thrift bailout regulations currently bar the RTC from selling property at below 95 percent of the market value in areas designated as having distressed real estate markets. This law was mandated to prevent "dumping," that is, the practice of selling large amounts of real estate in an area at below-market prices, which could be disastrous to an area already flooded with unsold property.

Financing Offered by the Resolution Trust Corporation

Although the RTC prefers cash offers on its properties, they will, in some cases, provide financing for the purchasers of RTC properties.

Buyers are required to pay a minimum of 15 percent of the purchase price as a down payment and the RTC will finance the remaining 85 percent. Interest rates, closing costs, and the length of time that the RTC will allow for the loan to be paid back, as well as the length of time it takes to close, are all set on a case-by-case basis depending on the price and location of the property. To date, set criteria exist which the RTC uses to qualify purchasers. RTC requirements concerning a purchaser's income-to-debt ratios and credit rating will also be determined on a case-by-case basis.

Tax Credits for RTC Property Purchasers

Currently, there is legislation under consideration that proposes a tax credit for investors who purchase RTC property. The tax credits would have to be structured both to save the government money and attract investors with the offer of tax benefits for properties purchased from the RTC.

This legislation would allow investors a credit on their federal tax bill (as much as a dollar-for-dollar reduction of what is owed at the bottom line). The purpose of this proposition is to provide incentive for investors to purchase RTC property. In certain cases this would allow purchasers to take tax credits over a 5-year period that is equal to as much as 80 percent of the equity they put into the property. After the property is sold, the RTC would be entitled to a percentage of the profit.

Resolution Trust Corporation Public Auctions

Occasionally, the RTC will hold public auctions to sell properties in its inventory. In many cases the auctions are held as an attempt to clear lower-value properties from the RTC inventory so that the agency can concentrate efforts on marketing its more expensive properties.

The RTC encourages real estate brokers to get involved in the auctions. Real estate brokers who register the successful high bidders at the auctions receive a commission of between 2 to 5 percent of the auctioneer's fee. (The auctioneer's fee averages 10 percent of the property's sales price.) Some of the RTC auctions will be "absolute auctions," with no minimum bid requirement; others will begin with an upset price. Contact numbers for auction sale information are listed in the RTC directory.

Working With the RTC as a Contractor

The FIRREA Act of 1989 has directed the RTC to use the public's expertise to help in the disposal of the RTC's acquired assets. To carry this out, the RTC offers contracting opportunities to the public. The contractors chosen by the RTC are asked to bid on specific tasks that deal with the contractor's area of expertise. The RTC seeks the public's assistance in a number of tasks. The major categories of expertise needed are as follows:

Asset Management
  Distressed loans
  Single-family property
  Hotel/motel
  Land
  Condominiums
  Mixed use

Property Management, Maintenance, and Leasing
  Property management
  Property maintenance
  Leasing
  Security service

Brokerage and Marketing
  Real estate brokers
  Opinion of value
  Marketing/sales
  Leasing

Planning and Construction
  Construction
  Real estate consulting
  Tenant finish out
  Construction consulting
  Environmental consulting
  Surveying
  Architectural/engineering consulting

Consulting Services
  Accounting, auditing, and financial services
  Asset analysis
  Financial investigation
  Property tax consulting
  Investment banking
  Real estate consulting
  Other consulting
  Loan administration

Title work

Asset management

Insurance

Legal services

Appraisal Services

Appraisals

Registering With the RTC as a Contractor

If you are interested in contracting with the RTC, the following paragraphs will explain the procedure that the RTC follows when it hires contractors.

First, the RTC registers private-sector contractors interested in working with the RTC. All firms wishing to work with the RTC must register first so that the RTC can understand a firm's expertise, capabilities, experience, and the geographic areas it is able to service. Ethical and confidentiality policies are also taken into consideration.

When a firm notifies the RTC of its desire to be considered as a contractor, the RTC will send out a contractor registration request form to be completed and returned to the RTC. Contractor registration request forms can be obtained by contacting one of the RTC's regional offices or the main headquarters in Washington, DC. The completed forms can be submitted to any RTC office. After the RTC receives the application, they review it and if the firm is in compliance with the RTC's requirements, it is notified that it has been accepted. The RTC is mandated to process all applications within 90 days of receipt of the completed forms. Congress has regulated the selection of contractors. The RTC will reject anyone who has been convicted of a felony, anyone who has been barred from participating in the affairs of an insured depository institution by any federal banking agency, anyone who has demonstrated a pattern of misconduct concerning insured depository institutions, and anyone who has caused a substantial loss (in excess of $50,000) to the federal deposit insurance funds. If it is determined that a firm is ineligible to provide contracting services, the firm will be notified within 30 days. All accepted contractors are entered by name into a contractor database. Future RTC contracts will be awarded only to firms that are registered in the RTC contractor database.

Bidding for Work as an RTC Contractor

When the RTC determines that it needs the help of the public sector in order to perform a certain job, the RTC compiles a *bid solicitation list* of contractors registered in the contractor database who have specific expertise in the applicable field. Firms on this bid solicitation list will receive a *Solicitation of Services* (SOS) from the RTC. This list contains a description of the services needed, the format in which the proposal should be submitted, the RTC's criteria for rating the proposal, and other details. The RTC does not limit the number of SOSs that a registered form may receive, but they will try to avoid constantly using the same firms.

The RTC chooses the contractor for the job through competitive bidding. The proposals are rated initially on technical merit, which includes the contractor's experience in the specific category of the needed service, the creativity in the proposed offer, the contractor's professional accreditations, evidence of written policies and procedures, and suitable accounting systems. The RTC will select the winning bidder based on these ratings along with the results of a reference check they will have done on the firm. The contract manager notifies all unsuccessful bidders within 90 days and, if requested, will provide an explanation of the facts involved in the RTC's decision. The contract is executed and signed by the RTC and the successful contractor.

The RTC retains the right to rescind any and all parts of a contract due to failure to disclose information, or to material changes in any representations made by the contractor. Other grounds for contract rescissions include personal or corporate conflicts of interest, nonperformance, or violation of the RTC's regulations.

The RTC upgrades and increases the efficiency of its policies and procedures for hiring contractors on an as-needed basis. This increases the effectiveness of the RTC's ability to serve the public's needs.

Procedures for Buying RTC Property

The RTC markets and sells its properties through RTC employees, or through real estate brokers that contract with the RTC. If you have purchased RTC property lists, you can contact the designated party for more information and for access to the property you're interested in. When you're ready to submit your offer to purchase an RTC property, the designated party can help you with the procedure.

If you don't have a list of RTC properties, but you're interested in a property that you know is owned by the RTC, you can approach an

RTC sales center directly and the center will provide you with information about the property and will refer you to an approved real estate broker used by the RTC.

Sometimes the RTC will give a real estate broker an *exclusive listing*, which is the exclusive right to market and sell a property. Real estate brokers who are interested in working with the RTC on *open listings*, those listings which involve properties that all brokers are invited to market and sell, are encouraged by the RTC to inform the sales center nearest them of their interest.

The Resolution Trust Corporation Offices

Main Headquarters

The RTC's main headquarters is located in Washington, DC.

Resolution Trust Corporation
Asset Management and Real Estate
  Division
801 17th Street, N.W.
Washington, DC 20006

(202) 416-7261 (Washington
  metropolitan area)
(800) RTC-4033 (outside calling
  area)

Regional Offices

The RTC has divided its property inventory throughout four regional offices. The regional offices oversee the consolidated and sales offices. The states that have been allocated to each regional office are subject to change. States in a given region will be reallocated as new properties are taken over by the RTC and as properties are sold.

Eastern regional office	States covered by the eastern regional office	
Marquis One Tower	Alabama	New Jersey
245 Peachtree Center Avenue, NE	Connecticut	New York
Suite 1100	Delaware	North Carolina
Atlanta, GA 30303	District of Columbia	Pennsylvania
(404) 225-5600 (Atlanta area)	Florida	Rhode Island
(800) 234-3342 (outside calling area)	Georgia	South Carolina
	Maine	Tennessee
	Maryland	Vermont
	Massachusetts	Virginia
	New Hampshire	West Virginia

(Continued)

Central regional office	States covered by the central regional office	
7400 W. 110th Street Overland Park, KS 66210 (913) 344-8100 (Kansas City area) (800) 283-3136 (outside calling area)	Alaska Arkansas Idaho Illinois Indiana Iowa Kansas Kentucky Louisiana Michigan Minnesota Mississippi	Missouri Montana Nebraska North Dakota Ohio Oklahoma Oregon Puerto Rico South Dakota Washington Wisconsin Wyoming
Southwestern regional office	States covered by the southwestern regional office	
300 North Ervay Tower 1, 23rd floor Dallas, TX 75201 (214) 953-2300 (Dallas area) (800) 782-4674 (outside calling area)	Texas	
Western regional office	States covered by the western regional office	
1225 17th Street Suite 3200 Denver, CO 80202 (303) 291-5700 (Denver area) (800) 283-7823 (outside calling area)	Arizona California Colorado Hawaii Nevada New Mexico Utah	

RTC Consolidated Sites and National Sales Centers

The RTC has organized *consolidated sites* and *national sales centers* to help in the acquisition and disposal of their properties.

The Consolidated Sites

The consolidated sites operate under the direction of RTC's four regional offices. The consolidated sites oversee savings and loans, asset sales, contracting operations, and conservatorships. The consolidated sites also assist in the liquidation of properties and assets. The consolidated sites are designed to be in areas where the RTC has a large concentration of assets, and it is expected that the number of consolidated sites will change over time as asset concentrations change.

The National Sales Centers

The national sales centers serve as clearing houses for all properties and other assets of failed savings and loans now in the RTC's hands. The sales centers are a reliable point of contact for buyers and real estate brokers to obtain information about available properties. Large transactions or those with national or international appeal will be handled by the main headquarters in Washington, DC. Every sales center maintains a complete list of RTC properties across the country.

Consolidated Sites and Sales Centers by State

The locations of the consolidated sites and sales centers used for each state are subject to change by the RTC.

Eastern region consolidated sites and sales centers	States covered	
Bayou Consolidated Office 100 St. James Street, Suite H Baton Rouge, LA 70802 (800) 477-8790 (504) 339-1000	Connecticut Delaware Maine Maryland Massachusetts New Hampshire	New Jersey New York Ohio Pennsylvania Rhode Island Vermont
Northeast Consolidated Office and Sales Center Valley Forge Corp. Center 1000 Adams Avenue Norristown, PA 10403 (800) RTC-NECO (215) 650-8500		

Southeast consolidated sites and sales centers	States covered
Southeast Consolidated Office P.O. Box 20587 Tampa, FL 33622 (813) 870-7000	Florida Puerto Rico

(Continued)

Southeast consolidated sites and sales centers	States covered	
Mid-Atlantic Consolidated Office and Sales Center 100 Colony Square, Suite 2300 Box 68 Atlanta, GA 30361 (800) 628-4362 (404) 881-4840	Alabama District of Columbia Georgia Kentucky North Carolina	South Carolina Tennessee Virginia West Virginia

Western region consolidated sites and sales centers	States covered	
Central Western Consolidated Office and Sales Center 2910 N. 44th Street Phoenix, AZ 85018 (602) 224-1776	Arizona Nevada	
Coastal Consolidated Office and Sales Center 1901 Newport Blvd., 3rd floor East Wing Costa Mesa, CA 92627 (714) 631-8600	Alaska California Guam	Hawaii Oregon Washington
Intermountain Consolidated Office and Sales Center 1515 Arapahoe Street Tower 3, Suite 800 Denver, CO 80202 (800) 542-6135 (303) 556-6680	Colorado Idaho Montana	New Mexico Utah Wyoming

Southwest region consolidated sites and sales centers	State covered
Gulf Coast Consolidated Office and Sales Center 2223 West Loop South Houston, TX 77027 (800) 879-8492 (713) 888-2900	Southeast Texas
Southern Consolidated Office and Sales Center 10100 Reunion Place, Suite 250 San Antonio, TX 78216 (512) 524-4700	West Texas
Northern Consolidated Office and Sales Center 4606 S. Garnett Tulsa, OK 74146 (918) 627-9000 (800) 456-5382	Oklahoma

Central region consolidated sites and sales centers	States covered
Mid-Central Consolidated Office 4900 Main Street Kansas City, MO 64112 (800) 365-3342 (816) 531-2212	Arkansas Kansas Missouri
Lake Central Consolidated Office and Sales Center 25 N.W. Point Blvd. Elk Grove Village, IL 60007 (800) 526-7521 (708) 806-7750	Iowa Minnesota Nebraska North Dakota South Dakota Wisconsin

RTC Directory of Services

The following offices have been created by the RTC to help the public in its quest to bid on properties or to work as a contractor for the RTC.

Office of Corporate Communication: (202) 616-7557. The Office of Corporate Communication plays a key role in helping the public understand the RTC's responsibilities and operations. They answer inquiries from the media and from the public, write press releases for the RTC, and work with the national news media to keep everyone abreast of the RTC's workings.

The Reading Room: (202) 416-6940. The people who work in the Reading Room disseminate rules and general information to the public concerning RTC policies and procedures. They are also the resource for information concerning the various divisions of the RTC and each division's duties.

The Office of Executive Secretary: (202) 416-7450. The Office of Executive Secretary handles requests for information from the public in accordance with the Freedom of Information Act. This office determines what information may be made public and what information must be kept confidential by the RTC.

Auction Sales Information: (202) 416-4200. The function of this office is to provide the public with information about upcoming auctions or asset sales.

Contractor Registration Requests: (800) RTC-4033. This office supplies information and contractor registration request forms for any person or firm interested in working for the RTC as a contractor.

7

Financing Foreclosures With Mortgages and Other Proven Methods

The golden rule for financing foreclosures is: *Never get involved in buying foreclosures at an auction unless you are prepared to have the money available to close, because you could lose your down payment.* The following financing methods are used by people who buy foreclosures. You must think them through and decide which method best meets your needs.

Financing a Foreclosure With a New Mortgage

One of the most popular ways to finance a foreclosure is by getting a new mortgage.

One of the largest purchases you will make in your life may be a mortgage loan. Just as you have spent countless hours choosing the property you wanted, you should now take an equal amount of time and care to choose a lender with a mortgage loan that best meets your needs. Don't make the mistake of applying for a mortgage financing with the first lending institution to catch your eye as you browse through the newspaper.

Whether you are a first-time homebuyer or you are purchasing the foreclosure as your third investment property, obtaining a mortgage loan can be as anxiety-producing as a hostile divorce proceeding. Although different states have different regulations for mortgage financing, the basic concept is uniform.

The Burden of Proof

The idea is to convince a lender to give you, the applicant, money, using real property as collateral. There are two requirements that all lenders share. First, the burden of proof lies with you to prove that you have sufficient income to repay the loan. Second, in the event that you default on your payments and the lender has to foreclose, it must be proved that the value of the property is enough for the lender to recapture its losses if the lender has to foreclose on you and sell the property at an auction. The entire mortgage procedure is aimed at defining and proving these facts.

Decisions, Decisions

You need to determine your plan for the future ownership of the property. This will help you to pinpoint the type of mortgage loan you are looking for. For example, if you intend to keep the property for more than 5 years, you may be better off with a fixed interest rate that will remain the same over the life of the loan. On the other hand, if you are buying the property with the intention of reselling it within 5 years, you should choose a variable (adjustable) rate which will be initially lower than a fixed rate, and then sell the premises *before* the periodic rate increases can decrease the cost effectiveness of this type of financing.

Basic Mortgage Types

Conventional Fixed-Rate Mortgages

The first type of loan we will look at has a fixed mortgage rate with fixed mortgage payments for the life of the loan. Conventional 30-year mortgage loans offer absolute certainty on housing costs. However, there is a higher initial rate than in most variable loans. Conventional 15-year mortgage loans offer lower rates than 30-year fixed-rate mortgages because quicker payoff of the loan allows a lender to put the money to work again sooner on someone else's new mortgage loan, at a higher interest rate. Lenders also like loans to be paid off quicker be-

15-year mortgage after 5 years	
Original mortgage amount	$50,000.00
Interest rate paid	11½%
Monthly payment (principal+interest)	$ 584.09
Total amount paid over 5 years	$35,045.40
Total interest paid over 5 years	$26,590.21
Total principal paid over 5 years	$ 8,455.19
Mortgage balance after 5 years	$41,544.81
30-year mortgage after 5 years	
Original mortgage amount	$50,000.00
Interest rate paid	12%
Monthly payment (principal+interest)	$ 514.31
Total amount paid over 5 years	$30,858.60
Total interest paid over 5 years	$29,689.90
Total principal paid over 5 years	$ 1,168.70
Mortgage balance after 5 years	$48,831.30

Figure 7-1. A comparison between a 15-year and a 30-year mortgage after 5 years.

cause it lessens the risk of the lender getting stuck with paying higher rates than they were charging their borrowers should loan interest rates skyrocket in the future. For example, on a $100,000 mortgage amortized over 30 years at a 10 percent interest rate, the monthly principal and interest payment would be $877.58. On the same $100,000 mortgage amortized over 15 years the interest may be lowered anywhere from one-quarter to one-half of a percent. At 9½ percent interest, the monthly principal and interest payment would be $1044.23, or an additional $166.65 per month. The 15-year mortgage borrower will pay higher monthly payments and will need to show more income than the 30-year mortgage borrower. Fifteen-year mortgages offer faster equity buildup and quicker payoff of the loan. If you were to freeze a $50,000 mortgage after 5 years, the differences between several aspects of a 15- and 30-year mortgage would be quite significant. Figure 7-1 is a comparison between a 15-year mortgage and a 30-year mortgage after 5 years.

The monthly payment for the 15-year mortgage is only $69.78 more per month, yet the amount applied toward reducing the principal loan is $8455.19 compared with a reduction of only $1168.70 on the 30-year loan. There is an obvious benefit in the 15-year mortgage, but many people are reluctant to commit to higher monthly payments for 15 years when they apply for a mortgage. For those who have chosen the 30-year loan with the lower monthly payment, the same effect of quicker reduction of the principal loan can be achieved by making extra payments during the year toward the principal loan, without committing to the higher monthly payment required for the 15-year loan.

FHA/VA Loans

Federal Housing Administration (FHA) and Veterans Administration (VA) loans are backed by the federal government. The benefits include lower down payment requirements and the fact that they are assumable with no prepayment penalties. These types of loans almost always require substantial points (prepaid interest) and may have application red tape and delays involved with approvals.

Balloon Loans

Balloon loans may offer lower rates and other favorable terms, especially when the loan is provided by the homeseller, but at the end of the mortgage term the entire remaining balance is due in a *balloon,* or *lump-sum payment,* requiring you to obtain new financing to pay this remaining balance at the required time. Some balloon terms provide for *interest-only payments.* This means that your payments are only for the agreed rate of interest. The interest is paid to the seller on a monthly or quarterly basis, and at the end of the loan term you have not reduced the mortgage balance.

Other balloon types provide for amortization over 15- or 30-year periods. The monthly payments would be higher because the monthly amount now includes payments to reduce the principal amount borrowed, in addition to the interest payments.

Balloon loans are most prevalent in situations in which the seller *holds the mortgage* or *holds paper,* which means that you pay the seller each month instead of a bank that's financing the loan. This type of arrangement benefits you if you are unable to obtain bank financing due to low provable income (you own a cash business), or if you have a bad credit rating. You also benefit by avoiding expensive closing costs such as points and origination fees which are usually charged by the lending institution in typical mortgage financing situations. Sellers benefit by having buyers for their property. In many cases you may choose to pay the asking price without trying to negotiate a lower price because this arrangement may be the only way you can achieve homeownership. At the end of the term, when the balloon payment of the remaining principal balance becomes due, you would get a mortgage loan from another source, usually a lending institution, and pay off the balloon loan. By this time you have had a chance to show provable income or clear up the credit problems that prevented you from initially getting a conventional loan.

Variable-Rate Mortgages

Variable- or adjustable-rate mortgages (ARMs) are loans on which the interest rate payment changes on a prearranged schedule. The most common variable terms are 6-month, 1-year, 3-year, or 5-year schedules. On the agreed anniversary of the loans, the payments are adjusted according to the prevailing rates. The benefit of this type of loan is that it generally offers lower initial rates than a fixed-rate loan, and it is usually assumable to new buyers. Adjustable-rate loans offer the possibility of future rate increases or decreases. In some cases, these loans may be convertible to fixed-rate programs after a previously agreed term. This type of loan has an increased rate risk because payments can be increased significantly in future years if interest rates skyrocket.

Graduated-Payment Mortgages

Graduated-payment mortgages are loans on which the payment increases by prearranged amounts during the first few years and then will stabilize at an agreed interest rate. This type of financing allows you to get the loan you can afford now, with the understanding that the rates will go up gradually, just as your income increases. The difference between this type of loan and an ARM, is that with a GPM loan you agree to the rate increases in advance instead of having to rely on changeable market rates, as you would with an ARM.

Comparing Lenders

When you are looking to get a loan, there are some key questions you need to ask in order to compare apples to apples. The method I found to be most effective involves a spreadsheet setup. Write the questions you want to ask across the top of the spreadsheet, and list the lending institutions you plan to contact along the side of the spreadsheet. Now you can call the lending institutions that advertise in your local newspaper. The lenders with the most expensive ads will not necessarily be the

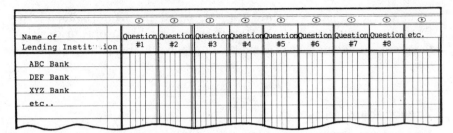

Figure 7-2. Sample spreadsheet setup for comparing mortgage programs offered by lending institutions.

ones with the best rates. Figure 7-2 illustrates a spreadsheet that is set up in this fashion. It can be used for your fixed-rate and adjustable-rate comparisons when you are shopping for a lender.

Key Questions to Ask a Lender

You will need to select some key questions to ask when you're comparing the mortgage loan products offered by lending institutions. Choose the questions that apply to your specific needs and write them across the top of your spreadsheet. After you have prepared your questions, list the names and telephone numbers of the lending institutions you have selected in the left column of the spreadsheet and start making your telephone calls to get the information. The spreadsheet format will help give you an organized overview of products available from the different lenders.

The following questions can be asked for both fixed- and adjustable-rate mortgages.

What is the bank attorney fee?   The lender's attorney is hired by the lending institution to represent its interests. The lender's attorney will review your application and confirm that the loan is acceptable. You have little control over what the fee will be, but if you have narrowed your choices down to two lenders, both with the same rates and other terms, and one lender charges $250 for its bank attorney's fee, while the other lender charges $750, you can either choose the lender with the lower fee or negotiate with the lender asking the higher fee in order to get it reduced. In any event, you may be surprised at the differences in fees for bank attorneys.

How long must you be at your present job to qualify for a loan with the lender?   Some lending institutions require you to be working for a certain length of time at a present job. Some lenders will be more flexible, and will take specific circumstances, such as a job transfer, into consideration.

Does the lender follow FNMA guidelines or portfolio its own loans?   When a lending institution gives mortgage money to you, they may then decide to sell the mortgage to the secondary market, and use the money they get from the sale to lend to new applicants. Federal National Mortgage Association (FNMA) is the largest secondary mortgage loans purchaser. If the lending institution sells to FNMA they may have different qualifying procedures than if they hold onto their loans and keep them in their own portfolio. There is a maximum mortgage amount that can be sold to FNMA. Loans that exceed FNMA mortgage loan amounts are called jumbo loans and the lender may have to hold these jumbo loans in its portfolios. For this reason, the qualifying criteria may be stricter or more lenient for loans that are kept in a lender's portfolio than for loans that are sold to the secondary market.

Can the loan rate be locked in?   If you want the assurance that the interest rate you are initially quoted remains the same and will not be increased by the time of the closing, you can ask for the rate to be *locked in.* The cost of the lock-in is of importance and it is wise to ask the lender what would happen if the rates go down. Would you get the benefit of the lower rate? Many times you can be penalized if you are locked into a rate and the prevailing rate lowers, because you may not be able to get the benefit of the reduced rate at the closing.

What is the prevailing rate?   The prevailing rate is the current interest rate the lender is charging for the loan.

How many points are being charged?   A point is prepaid interest and equals 1 percent of the mortgage loan being applied for. On a $100,000 mortgage loan, 1 point equals $1000.

Is there an origination fee, and how much is it?   An origination fee is an administrative fee that may be charged by a lender. Lenders do not always charge an origination fee. The fee can be anywhere from $100 to several points, and varies from lender to lender.

What is the application fee?   This is the fee charged to you by the lending institution when they open your file and begin the application process. The application fee may include charges for a credit report, an appraisal of the property, and other fees. It is also important to find out whether any part of the application fee is refundable if the mortgage application is denied, or if you do not accept the loan for any reason.

Is the mortgage you obtain assumable?   Loans that are assumable may be assigned by you to someone who might purchase the property from you later on when you decide to sell. This precludes them from having to qualify for their own mortgage and expedites the sale of your property. In the event that the mortgage is assumable, you will need to know the procedure involved for someone to assume it. In some cases, the person who assumes the mortgage must be requalified by the lender with the same strict guidelines that you were subjected to. Some lending institutions will permit a mortgage assumption for a nominal fee without any formal inquiries.

Is there a prepayment penalty?   A prepayment penalty is an extra charge to you if you pay off the mortgage before the end of the mortgage term (either through refinancing or selling your home). Federal laws may limit many prepayment penalty charges.

Does the lender escrow for property taxes and property insurance?   This means that the lender collects the payments for taxes and/or insurance from you each month as part of your mortgage payment and holds it in an *escrow account,* or reserve fund, for you. When the money is due, the lender will pay the taxes directly to the town or village as required. The lender will also pay the insurance company for your property insurance in the same manner. In this case, the lender is in control of the payments and can protect its interests by making sure the payments are made. You will need to know how many months of escrow are collected up front (at the closing) to help determine your closing costs. Federal laws limit the amount of reserves that can be asked for.

The following questions are recommended for adjustable-rate mortgage loans where payments fluctuate during the term of the loan.

What index does the lender use?   The index determines the bank's rate of borrowing, or the amount the lender is charged to put money out on the street to borrowers. The most commonly used indexes are the 6-month Treasury bill, the 1-year Treasury bill, and the Federal Home Loan Board. All lenders use one specific index. The current rate of the index can be found in most local newspapers and you can look it up yourself. Interest rates adjust according to the average of the index.

What is the lender's margin?   The lender's margin is the percent of profit a bank wants to make as profit above the index. This amount remains the same over the term of the mortgage. It is calculated as follows:

$$Index + Margin = Prevailing\ rate\ of\ interest$$

If the rate of borrowing (index) is 7 percent and the margin (profit) is 2 percent, then the rate you will be quoted is 9 percent.

When are the rates adjusted?   The most common adjustment periods are 6 months, 1 year, and 3 years. This means that your interest rate, and your monthly payment, will be adjusted on its 6-month, 1-year, or 3-year anniversary, depending on the plan you have chosen.

What is the *term cap*?   The *term cap* is the total amount the interest rates can go up or down during each adjustment period.

What is the *life cap*?   The *life cap* is the total amount the interest rates can go up or down during the life of the loan. For example, if you have a 30-year mortgage with a life cap of 16 percent, then the interest rate may fluctuate up to or below that amount, but it may *never* exceed it.

Is the mortgage convertible to a fixed-rate loan, and what is the procedure?   Adjustable convertible loans have become very popular because they allow you to start off with the lower initial interest rate of the adjustable loan and to convert to a fixed-rate loan later on. You will need to be given the procedure to follow and the costs involved with converting the loan to a fixed rate. You will also need information about how the fixed-rate amount will be determined. Some lenders will allow you to convert the loan after the first year for a small administrative fee, and other lenders will require you to wait for several years before you can convert the loan.

Is the loan negatively amortized?   This affects the loan's principal balance. When the prevailing rate (Index + Margin) goes above the maximum increase percent (term cap) allowed, the extra cost is passed on to you if the loan is negatively amortized. Usually you expect to reduce the principal balance of the loan (the amount you borrowed) as you make your monthly payments. If a loan is negatively amortized, the mortgage balance can increase, and your debt grows larger instead of smaller. For example, let's say you begin a loan with a 9 percent interest rate and you have a 1 percent interest rate cap yearly. At your 1-year anniversary, the index averages a 2 percent increase. Your new interest rate *should be* 11 percent, but because you have a 1 percent cap on the rate, your new interest rate for the next year is held at 10 percent.

In a regularly amortizing loan, the lender would absorb the 1 percent difference between the 11 percent you should be paying and the 10 percent you are capped at. In a negatively amortizing loan, however, the lender has the option of adding that 1 percent difference to your mortgage balance. You can either pay the negative difference in dollars before the new term begins, or the lender will add the amount to your mortgage balance. When the new monthly payment is calculated, your payments will be based on the increased mortgage balance instead of what you originally borrowed.

The answers you get to your questions can help you determine the mortgage that is best for you. If you have already purchased your foreclosure with cash that you borrowed from family and/or friends, you can get a mortgage loan on the property, based on its current value, and use the mortgage money to pay everyone back.

You may wish to use other, alternative methods for financing a foreclosure. Chapter 8 explains some of these alternative methods of financing in detail.

8

Alternative Methods for Financing Foreclosures

Using the Equity in Your Current Home

If you own a home that you have been living in for some time as an owner-occupant, then you probably have a good deal of equity built up in it by now. For example, let's say that 10 years ago you purchased a handyman's special for $60,000, put down $10,000 as a down payment, then got a mortgage loan to finance the remaining $50,000. If your house is located in an area where property values have appreciated, and if you've also made a number of repairs that have greatly increased your house's value, then you could estimate the house's current worth as, say, $150,000. The difference between your house's current value (in this example $150,000) and the remaining mortgage balance is called your *equity*.

If your current income and credit rating allow, you may refinance the property for up to 90 percent of its current value and reserve a portion of that cash amount to use for the foreclosure purchase. You may also choose to get an equity loan or a second mortgage based on the equity in your home and use that cash to buy the foreclosure. Of these choices, refinancing may appear most desirable, since banks will usually lend you more to refinance than to obtain a second mortgage or an equity loan. Also, your interest rate is usually lower on a refinance. Figure 8-1 shows you what a typical refinancing transaction might look like, and

Purchase price	$ 60,000
Down payment	− 10,000
Mortgage amount	$ 50,000 *(30 years at 10% interest)*
Current value	$150,000
Refinance	$135,000 *(90% of current value)*
Less: mortgage balance	− 45,450 *(approximately)*
Cash available	$ 89,550

Figure 8-1. A typical refinancing transaction for a 10-year-old mortgage.

Purchase price	$ 60,000
Down payment	− 10,000
Mortgage amount loan	$ 50,000
Current value	$150,000
Refinance amount	$105,000 *(70% of current value)*
Less: mortgage balance	− 45,450 *(approximately)*
Cash available	$ 59,550

Figure 8-2. A sample transaction for an equity loan or second mortgage.

similarly, Figure 8-2 presents a sample transaction for an equity loan or second mortgage.

When you're choosing one of these methods to finance your foreclosure, keep in mind that the amount a lender will allow you on a refinance may depend on your credit rating and income. But for equity loans, lenders usually concentrate more on the value of your house, and may pay less attention to your credit rating or income.

Obtaining Financing From the Owner of an REO

If you have decided to buy a foreclosure that is now bank-owned (an REO) or that has been taken back by HUD, the VA, or the GSA, you can usually get good financing terms directly from the lending institution or government agency that owns it. As I mentioned in Chapter 3, lending institutions are not in the business of managing property, and they would rather provide financing that would allow you to purchase the property than keep the property in their inventory where it would only cost them money to maintain. Cash offers are preferred, but if this is not possible, then the lender might agree to your financing terms.

Obtaining Financing From Foreclosing Lenders Before the Auction

In many cases, when a loan is in default, the lender holding the mortgage for the delinquent homeowner may agree to a straight assumption before the property goes to auction (see Chapter 4). The foreclosing lender may even agree to waive the late charges and back payments in order to avoid the expense of a foreclosure proceeding, and further loss of mortgage payments, in favor of having a new owner who is qualified, willing to assume the delinquent owner's loan, and able to pay the mortgage each month.

Getting Prequalified

When you purchase a foreclosure at an auction, you may be able to get financing from a bank within the 30-day period between the signing of the contract and the closing by getting *prequalified* by a lender before you bid. By prequalifying, you know how much you will be permitted to borrow based on your current income and credit rating. Lenders use the same procedures they would use to qualify you as a new applicant. Many lending institutions offer prequalifying services to prospective applicants. Be aware, however, that mortgage rates are higher for investors who will be renting the house out to others than for someone who will be living in the house as an owner-occupant. Also note that a lender will probably need access to the premises in order to check its condition before the mortgage is approved. There may be delays if, for example, utilities are not operating, the house is in need of a lot of repair work, or there are unfriendly occupants living in the house who won't allow a bank representative inside to inspect (or appraise) it. Because of the time involved in getting a mortgage approved, you can see why prequalifying may be a risky choice for financing your foreclosure since you will need to have the money within 30 days in order to avoid losing your down payment for a property purchased at an auction.

Buying With Partners

It has become increasingly popular for people to find partners to help purchase foreclosures. There are many wealthy professionals out there who have great credit ratings and lots of cash, but no time to do the legwork required in this sort of venture. If you have the time and the knowledge to acquire foreclosures, but your cash is limited, then you can offer your services as your contribution to the foreclosure purchase. Your job would be to find the property and to show the other partners why the property would be a good investment. The steps to take for finding the right property are detailed in the following chapters. You will need to decide whether you are interested in a longer-term partnership where the property would be rented out to tenants for an agreed period of time, or whether you and your partners wish to resell the property for a profit shortly after you purchase it.

This might be a good approach to take in order to obtain your first foreclosure. The profits you earn can be used toward building up enough money to be able to eventually purchase a foreclosure on your own. It is very important to remember that you need to build toward investing just as you would toward owning your dream house.

Realistically, most people are aware that owning the house of their dreams is something that happens over time. Most people begin with a "starter" home. From the equity built up when the house is sold, they move up to a better house, and so on, until they can afford the house they always wanted. The same realistic attitude is important for those of you who wish to buy investment property. Most of us don't have thousands of dollars available to go out and immediately buy a foreclosure with cash. But, just as you build toward the house you always wanted, you build toward having enough cash to purchase an investment property on your own. Partnerships are an ideal way to accomplish this.

There are many advantages built into this type of arrangement, such as the lower initial cost to purchase the foreclosure, the ability to share expenses, and if you are new at this endeavor, the security of knowing you have other people who share the same interest as you. An example of how such a partnership arrangement would look on paper is given in Figure 8-3.

Partnerships may be arranged in a variety of other ways, some of which could decrease the profit to you as organizer while increasing the profit to the other cash-contributing partners. For example, you could offer to repay the other partners for repair costs from your share of the

ROLES OF FOUR PARTNERSHIP MEMBERS

Partner 1:

Role: Organizer
Contribution: Expertise; no cash expenditure

Partners 2, 3, and 4:

Role: Financial
Contribution: $30,000 cash each
               $90,000 total cash outlay
Breakdown: $25,000 each toward purchase price
           $ 5,000 each toward repair costs

COST ANALYSIS OF PURCHASE OF FORECLOSURE PROPERTY

Purchase price	$75,000
Cost of repairs	+15,000
TOTAL COSTS	$90,000

The four partners decide to sell the property one month after its purchase. During this time, all necessary repairs have been made.

PROFIT ANALYSIS OF SALE OF FORECLOSURE PROPERTY

Sale price	$150,000
Each partner's share of profit	$ 37,500 *(4 equal shares)*

Profit for Each of the 3 Cash-Contributing Partners:

Share in sales price	$37,500
Share in initial purchase costs	(30,000) *(see above for breakdown)*
PARTNER'S TOTAL PROFIT	$ 7,500

Profit for the Organizing (Noncash-Contributing) Partner:

Share in sale price	$37,500
Share in initial purchase costs	0
PARTNER'S TOTAL PROFIT	$37,500

Figure 8-3. A sample partnership arrangement.

PURCHASE PRICE: $ 75,000
REPAIR COSTS: $ 15,000
SALE PRICE: $150,000

EACH PARTNER'S SHARE OF THE PURCHASE COST:

Each partner's contribution to the purchase price $25,000
Each partner's contribution to repair costs   − 5,000
EACH PARTNER'S TOTAL CONTRIBUTION $30,000

EACH PARTNER'S SHARE OF PROFIT ON SALE:
Sale price $150,000

Each partner's equal share of sale price $ 50,000
Less: Total original investment of each partner   − 30,000 *(see*
EACH PARTNER'S NET PROFIT $ 20,000 *above)*

Figure 8-4. Another sample partnership arrangement.

total profit. This would increase their profit by an additional $5000 each, but you would still net a considerable profit.

In another illustration of a partnership agreement (Figure 8-4), three people with equal cash contributions of $25,000 get together to purchase a property at an auction for $75,000 cash. They each put an additional $5000 into repairs, and then sell the property for $150,000 one month later. In this case, the total individual contribution of $30,000 makes each partner $50,000, or a profit of $20,000 − not bad for one month's work!

Using Credit Lines on Credit Cards

Using available credit lines on credit cards is one technique used by foreclosure purchasers when they wish to buy a foreclosure with cash. Remember that *credit lines are for the purpose of making money on the cash you use.* (You can buy luxury items later, with your profits!)

Property value	$100,000
Cash purchase price	$75,000
Credit lines used	$75,000
After closing:	
Obtain assumable mortgage for 90% of property value	$90,000
Repay credit lines used	$75,000
Sell to a buyer who will assume the mortgage	$90,000
Profit (before mortgage costs)	$15,000

Figure 8-5. Purchasing property using credit lines.

You will have to apply at lending institutions in order to obtain a credit line on credit cards. Be aware that in some states banks cannot legally charge an annual fee for credit cards. And make sure to find out the time period within which you must repay the amount you use so that you can avoid paying interest charges.

It is easier to obtain *many* lines of credit for *small* amounts that it is to get *fewer* lines of credit for *higher* amounts. Therefore, if you can get 100 credit cards with credit lines of $1000 each, you will have $100,000 available for buying foreclosures. Figure 8-5 illustrates how to purchase a property using lines of credit.

In order for credit line purchases to work most effectively, the following points should be considered:

1. You will need to pay back the credit lines within the required time period to avoid interest charges that will eat into your profit. This means that you will have to obtain your mortgage loan quickly.

2. The mortgage loan you obtain must be easily assumable to the subsequent buyer. Beware of assumable loans that have stringent qualifying procedures for the buyer who intends to assume the loan from you because this may delay the sale.

3. In most cases, you will need to be an owner-occupant living in the house in order to get the 90 percent financing you require.

4. In order to complete this transaction, you need to be able to sell the property to a buyer who will assume the mortgage. In a soft market, this may take some time.

5. A potential drawback may occur when you apply for lines of credit,

because the credit lenders will run a credit check on you as part of their qualifying procedure. This means that an "inquiry" will show on your credit report. When potential credit lenders see many inquiries on your account, they may decide that since you are applying for credit elsewhere, you are putting yourself in a position where you may become overextended should you use all the credit at your disposal. After a while, your credit line requests may be denied because of too many inquiries. On the other hand, if you have an intense desire to purchase foreclosures but no other available resources, this method may be your only means of taking advantage of some wonderful opportunities that you would otherwise have had to pass up.

Obtaining Hard-Money Loans

Another option for financing a foreclosure purchase is a *hard-money loan*. This is *not* "break-your-arm" financing by a loan shark. Rather, it is a financing tool based on the equity in the property, not usually on the good credit rating or high income of the borrower. This type of loan is usually available to applicants within a few days. Because of this, it is very desirable when fast cash is needed. The only drawbacks are the high points and high interest rates charged. Consequently, this form of financing is only recommended for a short period of time. You should replace it as soon as possible with a mortgage loan bearing a lower interest rate.

Building Wealth Through Contract Transfers

Another way people can build up enough money to purchase a foreclosure is through profits on contract transfers. In most cases, foreclosure purchases at auctions are transferable (assignable) because the successful bidder is expected to come up with cash for the purchase, and therefore, no financing is involved. The sale is not contingent upon the buyer's credit rating and the contract can be transferred to a new buyer, as long as the new buyer has the money required to close. Many investors make a lot of money by successfully bidding on a property and then transferring it to someone else before the closing. The new buyer will refund the original bidder's down payment plus the agreed-upon profit and will then become the new contract vendee (buyer).

As an example, let's assume you bid on a property that is worth

PROPERTY VALUE: $125,000		
PURCHASE VALUE: $ 75,000		
	Original bidder (you)	New buyer
Purchase price	$75,000	$80,000
Down payment	7,500	12,500
Due at closing	$67,500	$67,500

Figure 8-6. A sample contract transfer.

$125,000. You purchase it at the auction for $75,000. You give the referee $7500 as the 10 percent down payment. There is $67,500 due at closing. You transfer it before the closing to a new buyer. The new buyer gives you a down payment of $12,500, which reimburses your $7500 down payment plus a $5000 profit. The new buyer closes with $67,500 still due from your original contract. (See Figure 8-6.) The new buyer got a $125,000 property for $80,000 and made a great deal. You earned a quick $5000.

It is important to remember that this technique only works for cash purchases. When there is financing involved from the foreclosing lender (you purchase an REO and the bank who owns the property agrees to give you financing), then the loan will be contingent upon *your* credit history and income, and usually will not be transferable.

Another important thing to remember in contract transfers is that you must be certain that the new buyer is ready to come up with the cash for the closing. If the new buyer is not able to close, you may be held responsible and this may jeopardize your down payment. Clearly, then, it is to your best advantage to make *certain* that the cash is available for closing on the property. Otherwise, you may be left unprotected should you choose this method of purchasing a foreclosure.

Sitting on Hidden Treasure:
Whole Life Insurance Policies

Have you been holding a whole life insurance policy for a number of years? If you have, then chances are you've accumulated a good amount of cash in that policy by now. You have some choices to consider.

You can use the cash in your policy to buy a foreclosure. Or, you can borrow money from a bank using the cash in your policy as collateral and assign the ownership of the policy to the bank. Finally, you can take out a loan from a bank based on the policy's cash value. Using the cash you have accumulated as collateral, you can repay the loan and pay a fraction of the interest rate you would have paid on a typical personal or mortgage loan. Consult with your insurance agent for further details to determine if this method of financing is right for you.

9
Equity Sharing: Buying Foreclosures With a Partner

Equity sharing is a creative method of buying foreclosures. It is a form of copurchasing real estate and splitting the benefits during the owner-ship period. After the arrangement is completed, the house is sold and any financial gain is split as stipulated in the equity-sharing agreement. Although there are many variations in the utilization of this technique, the concept is basically the same. Equity sharing involves two partners. One partner is the *inside occupant*. The inside occupant lives in the house and generally puts up less money to purchase the premises. The other partner is called the *outside investor*. The outside investor supplies the larger portion of the down payment for the property purchase and does not live in the house. The example of equity-sharing used in this chapter involves an arrangement in which both partners have their names on the bond, mortgage, and deed.

In order to see why equity sharing has become so popular we must first address the needs of the parties involved.

The Typical Needs of the Owner-Occupant Homebuyer

A homebuyer's needs are influenced by many outside factors. Under normal market conditions, high interest rates and costly real estate prices keep homeownership potential at a minimum for many people. In addition, high rents keep many tenants from being able to save enough money to buy a home. A typical homebuyer needs a 10 percent down payment and anywhere from 5 percent to 10 percent of the mortgage amount for closing costs. These amounts can be prohibitive to people who wish to own their own homes.

The Needs of the Investor

In order to address the problems faced by today's real estate investors, we need to understand that an investor is someone who purchases real estate at below market prices using *as little of his or her own money as possible*. An investor will usually hope to get some kind of tax benefits from owning the property and will usually rent the premises to a tenant to help cover the carrying charges.

The first problem area for investors is tenants. When an investor rents out property to others, problems can arise if the investor does not take the landlording responsibility seriously. Inexperienced investors may think of real estate investing as a peaceful occupation, appropriate as a retirement job, with little to do other than collecting the rent and paying the mortgage. For most landlords living in the real world, this is not always the case. Typical headaches for landlords include:

Vacancies.   Your mortgage payment comes out of your pocket if there is no tenant living in your property to pay the rent.

Repair costs.   Unless you have arranged extraordinary leases, you as owner may be responsible for *everything* that goes wrong in your rental property. You also run the risk of repair bills incurred through vandalism or break-ins at your vacant rental house, or through damage caused by vacating tenants.

Tenant turnover.   Depending on the length of tenancy specified in your leases, you may have yearly turnover of new tenants, which can mean a new paint job, new alterations, and costly advertising for new tenants.

Rent collection.   You may have tenants who have a problem paying their rent on time, or even at all!

Deadbeat tenants.   Unless you have experience screening prospective tenants, and know the clues to tip you off, you may run the risk of renting to a "deadbeat" tenant who refuses to pay the rent and causes damage to the rental property.

Eviction. In the event that you may at some time need to evict a tenant, you should familiarize yourself with the eviction laws in your state in order to avoid costly lawsuits that can be brought against you for improperly ousting a tenant. I know an investor who illegally evicted his tenant by locking him out of the house because the tenant hadn't paid his rent for 6 months and the investor was about to lose the house to foreclosure. The landlord was arrested for violating the tenant's rights because the action he had taken against the tenant was an unlawful eviction procedure.

The second problem area for investors involves the 1986 tax revision laws that eliminated many tax shelter benefits that had been enjoyed by investors up to that time. A *tax shelter* occurs when losses from one investment are used to offset income from other sources and shelter (protect) it from income taxes. Another major change in these laws has to do with types of losses that can be used to offset types of income. *Active* income is earned when you work for it. At the end of the year you get a 1099 or a W-2 tax form from your employer for this type of income. *Passive* income, on the other hand, refers primarily to income earned from sources other than a job, such as income from interest or rent payments. Figure 9-1 is a brief summary of the differences in benefits shared by an investor with a yearly active income of $200,000 who owns investment property that has a $100,000 mortgage carrying a 10 percent interest rate.

	Investor's active (earned) income: $200,000 Mortgage amount: $100,000 at 10% interest rate	
	Before 1986 revision	After 1986 revision
Rent income	$10,000	$10,000
Cost of repairs	$12,000	$12,000
Mortgage interest	$10,000	$10,000
Depreciation	$ 5,500	$ 3,000
Total loss	$17,500	$15,000

Figure 9-1. Effect of 1986 tax-revision laws on an investor's active (earned) income.

As Figure 9-1 shows, the investor's rent income and cost of repairs remain the same, as does the mortgage interest deduction. However, before the 1986 revision, there was no limit on the number of second homes or vacation houses that the mortgage interest deduction could be taken on. Since the revision, mortgage interest deductions are now limited to the *first* and *second* homes *only*. Before the 1986 revision, the accelerated cost recovery system (ACRS) allowed properties to be depreciated over a 19-year period. After the revision, properties had to be depreciated over 27-1/2 years (31-1/2 years for commercial property) using the straight-line method of depreciation. This means that property is depreciated over a longer period of time, thereby lessening the yearly amount of deduction allowed.

Before the 1986 revision, the total loss of $17,500 could be deducted from the investor's active income, and if the investor owned several properties with deductions like this, he or she could offset the whole income and perhaps even show a loss! This is why real estate was such a tremendous tax shelter. Not only could an investor legally avoid paying income taxes, but he or she also owned an asset that was likely to appreciate in value and make even more money when it was sold. The 1986 revision now allows you to deduct up to $25,000 of losses from your adjusted gross income under $100,000. From $100,000 to $150,000 of income, the allowance is apportioned accordingly. In addition, the 1986 revision mandates that passive losses are to be deducted from passive income and can be carried forward until the loss is used up. As a result of the revision, many investors unloaded properties that no longer afforded them the tax benefits they had previously enjoyed. Consequently, there was a snowball effect as the demand for new building and construction lessened and rent amounts increased due to low supply and high demand for housing and tighter budgets for landlords.

The third problem area for investors is that high housing prices and high interest rates have eliminated *positive cashflow*. Cashflow is the money that flows into and out of the property. Normally the rent income, less carrying charges (mortgage payment, property taxes, property insurance) gives you the cashflow on a rental property:

Monthly rent income	$800.00
Monthly carrying	−$750.00
Positive cashflow	$ 50.00

In this case, the monthly rent income of $800, less the monthly carrying charges of $750, gives the investor a positive cashflow of $50 per month. In larger properties the carrying charges may also include repairs and other expenses. A *negative cashflow* will be effected if the monthly carrying charges exceed the rent income.

Figure 9-2 illustrates the differences between someone who wishes to buy a property as an owner-occupant (someone who will both own the

		As owner-occupant	As investor
Purchase price:	$100,000		
Yearly property taxes:	2,000		
Projected rental income monthly:	800		
Interest rate (%)		10	10½
Yearly earnings needed		$ 45,000	$ 40,000
Purchase price		100,000	100,000
Less: Down payment		(10,000) (10%)	(25,000) (25%)
Mortgage loan needed		$ 90,000	$ 75,000
Cash required:			
Down payment		$ 10,000	$ 25,000
Add: closing costs (10%)		9,000	7,500
Total cash needed		$ 19,000	$ 32,500
Monthly mortage costs:			
Mortgage information		$90,000/30 yr 10% interest	$75,000/30 yr 10½% interest
Principal and interest		$ 789.82	$686.06
Property taxes		167.00	167.00
Property insurance		50.00	50.00
PMI		25.00	–
Monthly mortgage payment		$1,031.82	$903.06
Monthly cashflow:			
Rental income		$ 800.00	
Less: Carrying		(903.06)	
Monthly negative		$ (103.06)	

Figure 9-2. Differences between an owner-occupant and investor who are buying the same property.

premises *and* live in them) and someone who wishes to buy an investment property and rent it to others (and who will *not* live there). The property used in Figure 9-2 is being purchased for $100,000. The yearly property taxes are $2000 and the projected rental income potential is $800 per month.

In this situation, we have an owner-occupant who is paying a 10 percent interest rate, and an investor who is paying the higher rate of 10-1/2 percent. Rates for investor mortgage loans are almost always higher than those for owner-occupant loans because there is a greater risk factor involved. When you're buying a property to live in, the lender qualifies *you* on your ability to pay the mortgage. On the other hand, when you're purchasing a property in order to rent it out to others, then the lender has no control over the qualifications of the tenant you will be selecting. If your tenant does not pay the rent and you can only afford to pay one of your mortgage loans, you are much more likely to pay the mortgage loan on the premises you reside in than the mortgage loan on the rental property. Thus, the risk factor is partially compensated for by higher interest rates and higher points charged for mortgage loans on investment property.

The owner-occupant needs to have earnings of approximately $45,000 compared to the investor who only needs $40,000 in earnings. This is because of the higher mortgage amount required by the owner-occupant. The owner-occupant requires a lower down payment because many lenders will give you 90 percent financing if you will live in the home. Most lenders will require at least 25 percent as a down payment from investors, once again, because of the greater risk factor.

The cash required to complete the purchase for the owner-occupant adds up to $19,000. This includes the 10 percent down payment of $10,000 plus closing costs of $9000 (estimated at 10 percent of the mortgage loan amount). The closing costs in this case include the owner-occupant's attorney fees, escrow charges for taxes and insurance, title fees, appraisal fees, and the bank attorney fees, as well as other ordinary closing costs. Closing costs vary from state to state, but in this example the 10 percent cost basis is used for both the owner-occupant and the investor. The investor will need to come up with $32,500. This includes the 25 percent down payment of $25,000 plus closing costs of $7500 (10 percent of the mortgage amount).

The monthly mortgage costs include the mortgage principal and interest based on a 30-year loan. The owner-occupant will pay a 10 percent interest rate, and the monthly payment includes principal, interest, property taxes, and property insurance. The owner-occupant's monthly payment will also initially include private mortgage insurance (PMI) costs of approximately $25 a month since less than 20 percent has been put down on the purchase price of the property. The total monthly cost to the owner-occupant is $1031.82. The investor will pay the higher interest rate of 10-1/2 percent, and the monthly payment also includes principal, interest, property taxes, and property insurance, although the investor will not have to pay a monthly PMI charge because of the 25 percent down payment. The investor's monthly mortgage amount comes to $903.06.

So now we have an owner-occupant who needs to come up with the large sum of $19,000 in cash, and we have an investor who needs to come up with an even larger sum of $32,500 in cash *and* (to add insult to injury) the investor will suffer a negative cashflow each month totaling more than $100! It is here that the many benefits of equity sharing come into play.

Equity Sharing to the Rescue

Equity sharing eliminates many of the aforementioned problems faced by homebuyers and investors. It is based on the premise that real estate will appreciate in value. It is used most effectively in a rising market so that there is low risk to both parties. Also, the need for housing and the pride of ownership will always exist.

If two individuals buy a property as co-owners and use an equity-sharing arrangement, they will each get the best of both worlds.

The inside occupant (we'll call this partner the *insider*) can now achieve homeownership for a much smaller dollar investment or cash outlay than if he or she purchased the property individually. The insider has enough income to support the monthly payments, but does not have enough money for the down payment and closing costs.

The outside investor (we'll call this partner the *investor*) also benefits from equity sharing. For the investor, management and overall risk are minimal since the tenant is also an owner. The investor wants the tax benefits and profits from the property, not a tenant who will call at night with problems.

Using the concept of equity sharing, we will see the numbers in Figure 9-2 start to change. Equity sharing allows two parties to purchase the property, and in this fashion both partners get each other's benefits while eliminating most of the detrimental aspects involved.

Let's now take a look at some of the elements listed in Figure 9-2, and see how some of the dollar amounts given there are affected.

Interest. The investor can have the benefit of the lower interest rate previously available only to an owner-occupant (10 percent instead of 20 percent) since the partner (the insider) will be living in the house.

Earnings. The insider does not have to show as much income as he or she would normally because the investor is now a coborrower.

Down payment. The investor gets the benefit of the lower amount of down payment needed (10 percent instead of 25 percent). This purchase is no longer considered an investment because one of the partners (the insider) will be living in the house. Through equity sharing, both partners get the benefit of the insider's lower down payment requirement. Remember, investors like to use as little of their own money as possible!

Negative cashflow. Negative cashflow for the investor is eliminated since the insider's "rent" each month will equal the carrying charges for the property.

What You Need to Agree Upon

As I said earlier, the beauty of equity-sharing arrangements is the flexibility of the terms of the agreement. There are some basic points that need to be agreed to from the outset, and both an attorney and a tax advisor should be consulted by all involved parties. Here are some of the items you will need to agree on in order to satisfy everyone's needs and to protect the interests of both partners.

The purchase price limits. The price of the property to be purchased in the venture must be determined and agreed on initially by both the insider and the investor since both parties will be co-owners.

The percent of down payment and closing cost contribution. The insider and the investor must agree to the split of the down payment amount and closing costs that each party will contribute. In some cases, the investor agrees to pay the entire down payment and closing costs, and in some cases the agreement is a 50-50 split in which each party pays 50 percent of the amounts needed. Also commonly used is a 60-40 split in which the investor pays 60 percent of the down payment and closing costs and the insider pays 40 percent. A 70-30 split, an 80-20 split, and a 90-10 split may also be arranged. Figure 9-3 illustrates a 90-10 split in which the investor contributes 90 percent of the down payment and closing costs and the insider contributes 10 percent. The purchase price is set at $100,000 and a 10 percent down payment is required. Total closing costs are estimated at 10 percent of the mortgage amount of $90,000.

In Figure 9-3 we can see that $17,100 is a much more palatable sum of money for the investor to come up with than the $32,500 amount shown in Figure 9-2, which was the amount the investor originally needed to purchase this property on his or her own.

The insider needs only $1900 in this situation, as compared to the much higher $19,000 he or she needed in Figure 9-2 to purchase his or her own property.

The agreed-upon contribution responsibility does not have to be the same for both the down payment and the closing costs. For instance, both parties may decide that the investor will pay 90 percent of the down payment and the insider will pay the remaining 10 percent, and that they will share an equal 50-50 split as their contribution rate toward the closing costs.

The contribution split of the carrying charges.   In some cases the carrying charges (mortgage payment of principal, interest, property taxes, and property insurance) are equal to the rent, or monthly amount paid

Purchase price:	$100,000	
Down payment required:	$ 10,000	(*10% of purchase price*)
Mortgage needed:	$ 90,000	
Closing costs needed:	$ 9,000	(*10% of mortgage needs*)

	Investor*	Insider*
Down payment contribution	$ 9,000	$1,000
Closing cost contribution	+8,100	+900
Total cash contribution required	$ 17,100	$1,900

*Investor pays 90% and insider pays 10% of the total of each contribution needed.

Figure 9-3. Illustration of 90-10 down payment split under an equity-sharing arrangement.

for by the insider. This way the insider is responsible for paying the total monthly mortgage costs for the property. Again, there are no hard and fast rules about the way the carrying charges are split. It may be agreed that the insider and investor will share the carrying charges equally. Internal Revenue Service regulations may require that the insider pay what would be considered rent for using the half of the house that the investor owns, since technically both parties own the property and the insider is occupying both his or her half and the investor's half. For example, two partners may buy a property for $100,000 with a down payment of $10,000. There is a mortgage balance of $90,000 amortized over 30 years at a 10 percent interest rate. The monthly mortgage payment for principal and interest is about $790. In a typical arrangement, the insider would write a check to the mortgage lender for $395, which is half of the $790 mortgage payment. At the same time, the investor would write a check for the other half. In addition, the insider would write another check for $395 payable to the investor to reflect the rent for the half of the home that the investor owns but the insider occupies. In such a case, investors may be required to report the amount paid to them by insiders (for the use of their half of the property) as rental income. In some cases the IRS may disallow some of the income tax deductions taken by either party if fair market rent isn't paid. For this reason and many others, a tax adviser should be consulted by both parties so that the entire equity-sharing arrangement is structured for maximum protection and benefits.

The amount of homeowner's insurance coverage.   Both parties must agree to the amount of homeowner's insurance coverage needed to protect the property. Usually, the insider will get the insurance policy and the investor will be named as "also insured."

The amount of life insurance coverage.   In many cases the parties may agree that there should be a life insurance policy taken by each party in an amount that covers the mortgage balance. In the event that one of the parties dies, the property will be paid off and the equity benefits shared with beneficiaries, as previously agreed to.

The contribution responsibility for repairs and other cash expenses. Some of the most popular variations of expense responsibility include:

1. Both parties share all cash expenses (repairs, insurance, property taxes).

2. The investor pays all cash expenses and the insider pays a higher rent.

3. The insider pays all cash expenses and carrying charges and the investor pays a larger portion of the down payment and closing costs.

The sharing of tax benefits.   IRS Code 280A specifically addresses regulations regarding equity-sharing arrangements. In order to qualify for many of the tax benefits of equity sharing, there are some basic rules that must be followed. The contract between the parties must be in writing, not just a verbal agreement. In order for both parties to take deductions, the contract may have to state that both parties will have ownership interest for at least 50 years. This does *not* mean that the two partners have to keep the property for 50 years; in fact, most equity-sharing arrangements call for the venture to end within a 3- to 5-year period. Either party may dissolve the contract at whatever time was initially agreed upon, but the intended term of the contract may have to be stated at 50 years in order to claim the tax deductions.

The investor is the only partner allowed the depreciation deduction because the investor is the owner who is not living in the property.

The agreement for the split of the mortgage interest deduction can be determined by each partner's percent of contribution to the payments during the year. For example, if each party contributes half of the mortgage payment, as in the earlier example (where both parties pay half the monthly payments for the mortgage principal and interest), then each party could claim 50 percent of the mortgage interest deduction. Again, the contribution and deduction percentages are flexible and should be prearranged in the equity-sharing agreement so that both partners' needs are specifically understood and satisfied.

The contribution split for operating expenses.   Usually the insider is responsible for expenses involving utilities such as heat, electricity, and water since it is the insider who will be living in the house and using the utilities.

The split of the built-up equity when the arrangement ends.   The value of the property above the mortgage balance is the *equity* in the property. One of the most important aspects of equity sharing to be agreed upon between the partners is the share of the equity that each partner will be entitled to at the end of the partnership. Sometimes this can be dictated by the contributions each partner has made at the beginning of the partnership. For example, if there was a 50-50 split of the initial contribution for down payment and closing costs, then the agreement may call for a 50-50 split of the equity that has been built up during the ownership of the property. If the value of the property when it is sold is $150,000 and the remaining mortgage balance is $90,000, then the equity in the property is $60,000. Therefore, in a 50-50 split, each partner would be entitled to $30,000. This same concept can be applied to the 90-10 split used in Figure 9-3. In that case, the investor would be entitled to 90 percent of the equity and the insider would be entitled to 10 percent. Some equity-sharing agreements call for one or both partners to be reimbursed for their original outlay of the down payment and closing costs and for a split of the remaining equity according to the percentages in the agreement.

The importance of the method used to estimate the property value is obvious. Usually, both parties obtain independent appraisals from competent, acceptably qualified appraisers and use the average of the two appraisals to determine their property's value.

The buyout term.   The equity-sharing agreement must provide for the venture's end. As stated previously, the most common equity-sharing arrangements last for a term of from 3 to 5 years. At that point, the co-ownership partnership will be terminated through a prearranged method. The most common methods include a buyout agreement between the two partners in which one of the partners has to buy out the other partner, that is, one partner buys the other partner's interest in the partnership. In this case, the partner who buys the property from the other partner will retain full title and have complete ownership of the property.

The other common method of buyout provides for the property to be sold to someone other than the partners and, based upon a prearranged agreement, the proceeds to be split between the partners.

If the agreement calls for one party to buy out the other party, the terms of the buyout should be agreed upon at the outset. In a buyout arrangement, the partner who will be buying pays the other partner the agreed-upon percent of the equity split, and the buyout is completed. There should be an agreement about the method that will be used to determine the buyout amount, as well as the source of funds that will be used to pay the agreed amount. Will the buying partner have to obtain a new mortgage loan and pay off the original loan so that the selling partner is no longer a party to the original mortgage obligation? Will the buying party pay the other party off with cash, and in this case, will the lending institution release the selling partner from the mortgage obligation? These details are important because later on, if the partner who has bought out the other partner defaults on the original mortgage agreement, the selling partner, whose name might still be on the mortgage note or bond, may be held responsible for the debt even though he or she is no longer an owner.

If the agreement calls for the premises to be sold to someone other than either partner, there are some details that can be prearranged in the original contract. There should be a decision about how the sale price will be determined and the medium through which the property will be sold. For example, will the house be listed for sale exclusively with one particular real estate broker, or as an open listing, so that only the real estate broker who sells the property will get the commission? Or will the partners try to market and sell the property themselves? Other decisions include the commission rate to be paid to the broker who sells the house, and the length of time that the listing will be given to a real estate broker.

Other Standard Clauses in Equity-Sharing Contracts

Standard clauses in equity-sharing contracts include, but are not limited to, the following:

Prevention of future borrowing. There should be some agreement between the insider and the investor that no future borrowing is allowed, and that the property may never be used as collateral on a loan that either partner obtains individually. There should also be an agreement to prohibit a second mortgage on the property since this would use up the equity that is being built up.

Option defaults. There should be some stipulation in the contract about the penalties that will be incurred should the party who has agreed to buy out the other party fail to fulfill that obligation.

Payment defaults.   There should be an agreement about the penalties that will arise should either party default on the obligations by failing to pay carrying charges, mortgage payments, other expenses, and so forth.

Dispute remedies.   Both parties should agree on the methods they will use to settle disputes that may arise during the time they will be equity-sharing partners. These methods include, but are not limited to, the use of arbitration boards and/or litigation through the court systems.

The Risks Involved in Equity Sharing

As with any endeavor that involves an investment of money, there are always risks that are taken. Since equity sharing is based on the premise that property values are appreciating, deflation is one potential risk. Deflation, however, is usually a temporary state of affairs, and since the need for housing continues to rise with the times, most experts feel that real estate is a most viable investment.

If either partner defaults on the agreement, there is the chance that the other partner may have to be responsible for the payments involved. The equity-sharing partnership may have to be terminated and the property sold, but both parties would get the benefit of the equity increase that will have occurred during the agreement. As the term of ownership lengthens, the risks are minimized because the property is appreciating and the mortgage balance is being reduced, thereby increasing the equity in the property.

Should there be a need to sell the property as a remedy for default, both parties should recover their original investment, in addition to the equity that has built up, and both will have enjoyed the tax benefits of their arrangement.

A Great Method to Buy Foreclosures

Equity sharing is a great method for two partners to use as a source of financing and owning a foreclosure. The concept works when the foreclosure is purchased at a below-market price and the chances for appreciation are greater.

The following example is a common situation in which parents and their child wish to set up an equity-sharing arrangement in order to purchase a foreclosure. The parents are looking for a tax shelter and the child, although having a good income, has no cash saved for the down payment and closing costs.

The parents and child purchase an REO from a lending institution for $100,000. They will make a 10 percent down payment, and the lending institution has agreed to give them 90 percent financing for 30 years at a 10 percent interest rate. The parents will pay 100 percent of the down payment and closing costs. The child will pay all the monthly carrying charges and will be responsible for completing any repairs. The parents will get 100 percent of the depreciation as a tax benefit and they will split the mortgage interest deduction 50-50. The parents and child have agreed to sell the property in 5 years and they will split the equity 50-50 after the sale. The property taxes are $2400 per year. The parents will be the partners who are considered the investors, and the child will be the insider who will live in the house. Figure 9-4 illustrates the way this will work.

After 5 years, if the property appreciates at the rate of 5 percent yearly, the new value will be $135,000. The mortgage balance would be approximately $88,000. If the property is sold for $135,000, the equity proceeds would be $47,000, which would give each of the partners (parents and child) $23,500. In tabular format, this is:

Property value	$135,000 (*5% appreciation yearly*)
Less: Mortgage balance	(88,000) (*approximately*)
Equity proceeds	$ 47,000
Split	$ 23,500 each

The parents received $23,500 from their $19,000 investment and got back $4500, which comes to approximately 4 percent yearly return on their investment. They will also get depreciation and mortgage-interest deductions on their income taxes. The child will now have $23,500 to use as a down payment on another property and will be able to buy that property on his or her own.

Let's look at another example of an equity-sharing arrangement, this time between a contractor and an investor. The contractor will be the insider, and will live in the house while making repairs. The contractor's equity-sharing partner is the investor. The investor will be responsible for the initial cash outlay for the down payment and closing costs. The

Purchase price:	$100,000
Mortgage amount:	$90,000 (*10% interest for 30 years*)
Closing costs:	10% of $90,000 mortgage ($9000)
Yearly property taxes:	$2400
Down payment contribution:	100% (*paid by parents/investors*)
Closing cost contribution:	100% (*paid by parents/investors*)
Carrying charges:	100% (*paid by child/insider*)
Repairs:	100% (*paid by child/insider*)
Tax benefits:	Parents get depreciation
	Mortgage interest is split 50-50
Buyout time:	5 years
Equity split:	50-50

	Parents	Child
Down payment	$10,000	–
Closing costs	9,000	–
Cash outlay	$19,000	0
Monthly carrying:		
Principal/interest	–	$ 789.82
Property taxes	–	200.00
Property insurance	–	50.00
PMI	–	25.00
Total monthly carrying	0	$1,064.82

Figure 9-4. An equity-sharing arrangement between parents and their child.

contractor will contribute $19,000 worth of repairs to the property. Using the same conditions as in Figure 9-4, the two partners will purchase a handyman's special REO from a lending institution for $100,000, and the lending institution will give the same financing terms of $90,000 amortized over 30 years with closing costs of $9000 and a down payment of $10,000. The contractor has materials and will contribute the labor as his or her part of the deal. The investor will pay the down payment and closing costs. The contractor has enough income to support the required repair costs of $19,000, but no money for the initial down payment and closing costs. In this situation both partners agree to an

immediate sale after the repairs are made, and the repairs are expected
to be completed quickly.

After repairs are completed, the property's value will be considerably
higher. In this case, we will assume that $19,000 worth of repairs could
raise the value of the property from $100,000 to $150,000. The mortgage balance would pretty much remain the same because of the quick
sale. Here's how things would work out:

Purchase price	$100,000
Sale price	150,000
Mortgage balance	90,000
Proceeds	60,000
Split	30,000 each

A $30,000 return on a $19,000 investment yields a 57.9 percent return for the investor if the property is sold quickly. In this case the
partners would need an ironclad agreement, including what repairs
will be made by the contractor as his or her contribution. You would
also need to make sure that the lender will not charge a prepayment
penalty for paying off the loan as expected within the first couple of
months.

Finding a Partner for Equity Sharing

As an inside occupant who is looking for an investor as a partner, you
should do the following:

1. Make an appointment with your tax advisor or attorney to work out
   a plan that enhances your monetary needs. You will need to determine how large a monthly payment you can afford to make in order
   to determine the purchase price range of the property you will be
   looking for.

2. To attract investors, put an ad in your local newspaper, such as:
   **"Only $19,000 buys 90 percent ownership of income property. In-
   vestor's dream: 90 percent profit when sold—0 percent headaches
   of landlording. Positive cashflow monthly. Call Mr. Averageson at
   (212) 555-1000."**

3. Look in the classified section of your local newspaper under such headings as "Money to Lend." Many times investors with money to put into this sort of venture will advertise there.

4. When you find an investor to work with, set up an appointment to discuss your intentions and to outline a plan of action regarding the cost of the property you wish to purchase together and the contributions you will each be comfortable making. You will need to discuss the tax deductions, the monthly payment setup, and the buyout terms. Both parties should bring their attorneys or tax advisors to this meeting in order that everyone's intentions may be made clear and everyone's interests may be protected.

5. Inspect and select the property that is right for you and enter into a formal contract between the seller and you and the investor.

6. File your mortgage application, close, and move in.

The outside investor might follow these steps in order to find an inside partner:

1. Consult your tax advisor or attorney to review the tax ramifications involved in equity sharing, as well as your capital requirements and availability of funds.

2. Put an ad in your local newspaper to attract an insider, as follows: **"No cash down buys 10 percent ownership of 8-room high-ranch in Any County, USA. Payments each month equal rent of $_____. No need to qualify for a mortgage. Call Ms. Welloff at (201) 555-2000."**

3. When you find an insider who will work with you, it may be advisable to ask him or her to provide a credit report so that you can see if he or she would make a creditworthy partner. Since you will be the partner bearing the greatest risk because you will be putting up the greater amount of capital, doing this will help you to protect your interests. You will also need to discuss your intentions regarding the equity-sharing terms of your agreement. Therefore, you may wish to include the insider's attorney or tax advisor in the meeting, as well as your own.

4. When you find the property that is right for you, proceed with the contract between the seller and you and your partner.

5. File the mortgage application and close on the property.

Equity sharing satisfies the needs of an investor who wants to buy a foreclosure but who wants the added security of a good tenant. It also satisfies the needs of someone who would like to buy a foreclosure as an owner-occupant, but who does not have all the necessary cash to buy it alone.

10
Choosing the Right Property: What You Don't Know *Can* Hurt You

You will need to inspect the properties you are interested in and ask questions of certain people and agencies before you attend any auctions or make any written offers. The results of your inspection, combined with the answers you receive to some pertinent questions, will help you accurately determine your costs when you purchase a foreclosure. This chapter will detail the preliminary preparations for choosing the property that is right for you and for determining whether that property is worth pursuing.

Access to the Property

You will need to contact the referee or designated authority for access to the premises. You may be told, "You can inspect the property on Saturday at 3:00," or you may be told, "If you can get past the pit bull and the guy with the shotgun, be my guest!" In any event, be prepared to make your inspection.

The Preliminary Inspection

Take pictures of and notes about the property you're inspecting. If you will be inspecting five or six properties, the most important thing you can do is to take *specific* notes about each one. So be sure to bring a notepad. You will never be able to remember all the details of every property unless you write down as much information as possible. Attach all the pictures you take of every property to each individual inspection sheet you prepare. The important things to look at (in addition to the cosmetic appearance and the plumbing, heating, and electrical systems) are the structure itself plus any improvements, the sheds, the inground pool, the detached new garage, any extensions that have been added, and anything else that may have been added to the property. For expediency in picture taking, an instamatic camera is recommended. (Imagine shooting an entire roll of film just to find out later that it hasn't developed properly so that you have to go back and reshoot everything all over again!) A flashlight is also recommended because in many cases the electrical system will have been disconnected once the property becomes vacant.

Keep the pictures and the notes you have taken accessible so that you may refer to them when you're contacting the various parties that I'll be mentioning throughout this chapter.

A Lifesaving Safety Tip for Inspections

When you're inspecting vacant properties as part of your preliminary preparations for bidding, please keep in mind this lifesaving safety tip: *Never enter a vacant house carrying a lit cigarette.* There may be a gas leak of which no one is aware (since no one lives there), and a lit cigarette could cause an explosion of disastrous, life-threatening proportions.

Protect Yourself

Another safety tip is illustrated by my own personal experience. After we inspected a vacant prospective foreclosure, my assistant noticed something on my clothes. I looked down and saw hundreds of small dots all over my white skirt. (It's a good thing it was summertime and that I was wearing a light-colored skirt!) Then, I realized the itching I was feeling wasn't imaginary, and that those little dots were moving! *Fleas!* Hundreds of fleas all over me! It seemed at the time that the fleas were waiting for just such a pair of legs to present themselves for dinner. If my assistant hadn't noticed my skirt, my car, my dog, and, consequently, my home would have become infested. Finding yourself in such a situation is a nightmare, and can be dangerous for people who are allergic to flea bites. The point is, remember to bring insect repellent and to wear protective clothing or at least put rubber bands around the bottom of your pants legs in order to keep these annoying creatures from crawling under your garments..

Once Is Not Enough

I suggest that you visit the properties you're interested in inspecting at different times of the day and in different weather conditions. Does the property flood during a heavy rain? Is the area surrounding the property a local hangout for noisy teenagers? Is the property near a body of water that might cause flooding or other problems at high tide? (One lender told me about an REO owned by his bank. The property was located on a canal. It was sold every morning, and went back on the market for sale again every night. People came to inspect the property in the morning, liked it, and put down a deposit. When they came back later in the afternoon—after high tide—they found fish all over the front lawn and rescinded their offer!) Is there a railroad line nearby, and when the train comes through does it shake the pictures off the wall and transform the bath water into a whirlpool? The result of your inspections of the same properties at different times of the day and during different weather conditions may result in some very different findings that will save you a lot of headaches in the long run.

Ask the Nineteen Magic Questions

□ **What form of down payment is required?**

Contact the referee or the foreclosing lender's attorney and ask what form the down payment must be in. Usually you'll be told that the down payment must be in the form of a certified check, attorney's check, or money order. Cash may also be acceptable in some cases.

□ **When is the closing date?**

Ask when the closing date will be. Usually in foreclosure auction situations, the closing must be completed within 30 days of the day that the property was awarded to the high bidder at the auction and the contract signed. On the other hand, if you are purchasing an REO and the bank that owns the property agrees to provide financing, then the closing date will be set by the bank once the financing is approved. In this case the 30-day closing deadline would not be applicable.

□ Will I lose my down payment if I fail to close?

Ask whether the down payment is redeemable (refundable) if you have purchased the property at an auction and are unable to close in the 30-day period stipulated in the referee's contract. In most cases, the down payment will *not* be redeemable if failure to close is the fault of the high bidder. But if the foreclosing lender is unable to close for some reason, there is a possibility that the down payment might be redeemable. Causes for redemption may include, but are not limited to, improper service of legal documents on the delinquent borrower at the time the foreclosure action first began; additional liens and judgments that have been discovered which were accidentally omitted from the upset price (which could cause the upset price to be substantially raised after the fact), or the foreclosing lender's inability to provide the necessary legal documents (Torrens title). In the event that the down payment is redeemable for any reason, you would also want to know how long it would take you to recover your money.

□ Is there a Torrens title or a regular deed, and is it available?

Ask if the property has a regular deed or a Torrens title and ask whether it is available. As discussed previously, this information would be in the title report ordered by the foreclosing lender's attorney when the foreclosure action was first begun.

□ Is the contract transferable?

Ask if the contract is transferable. In the event that you are purchasing the property at an auction, as the successful high bidder you will be expected to pay for the property with cash and no financing is given by the referee. Therefore, the sale is not contingent upon your credit rating and can be assumed by another buyer as long as the other buyer has the cash required to close. In a case where you are buying an REO and the bank will be providing financing, you will not be able to assign the contract to anyone else. The financing approval will be contingent upon your ability to pay since you are the one applying for the financing.

☐ Who is responsible for the protection of the premises between the contract and closing dates?

Ask who is responsible for the protection of the premises after the contract is signed and up through the closing date. In most cases the foreclosing lender cannot protect the premises or give any guarantees about its condition if there are people occupying the property. If the property is vacant however, the foreclosing lender's insurance should cover any additional damages that occur between contract and closing.

☐ Who is responsible for major structural repairs?

Ask who is responsible for major structural repairs. If you are purchasing the property at an auction, in most cases, you are responsible. Remember, you are purchasing the property in as-is condition. If you are purchasing an REO or a property that is owned by a government agency, however, you may be able to get monetary assistance for repairs. I was once involved with an REO purchase in which the bank that owned it issued a $500 credit at the closing toward repair of a collapsed cesspool.

☐ What is the status of any current occupants?

Ask about the status of any current occupants. In the event that you successfully bid on the property at an auction and there are people currently living in the property, you will probably be responsible for the eviction procedures once you are the new owner. Perhaps the occupants have already advised the foreclosing lender that they are in the process of moving out voluntarily. This may help you to be more accurate when you figure out the amount you will bid on the property because you can eliminate eviction costs from your bidding calculations. If you are purchasing an REO, in many cases the property has already been vacated. Many lenders that have taken REOs into their inventory have legally evicted any occupants as a prerequisite to putting the property on the market.

□ **Is prepossession allowed prior to closing if I am in
   contract?**

Ask if prepossession is allowed between the contract and the closing,
once you're the successful high bidder. If the premises are vacant, you
may want to begin making repairs in order to rent or sell the property.
If the property is in good enough condition, you may want to move in
yourself. Possession may also be granted for REOs. Many lenders find
this to be in their best interest because it can help them avoid the vandalism that might normally occur in a vacant property. You must confirm that the property is properly insured for losses sustained. Many
times you will be required to provide your own property insurance if
you are going to be granted prepossession.

□ **Does the original owner's "right-of-redemption"
   period survive the auction?**

Ask if the right-of-redemption period survives the auction. In a bank
foreclosure in some states the previous owner's right of redemption is
over once the bidding begins. In other states, the owner's right of redemption may exceed the auction, which means that even after the
property is awarded to someone else, the previous owner still has a limited time to pay the upset price and redeem ownership.

□ **Are there any additional liens or judgments
   attached to the premises?**

Ask if there are any additional liens or judgments attached to the premises for which you would be held responsible, in addition to the purchase price. This question is especially important in auction situations if
you are the successful high bidder. In most REO cases the bank clears
the title once the property comes back into its inventory by paying off
the outstanding liens and judgments. In an auction situation, however,
this may not be the case and you may be responsible for payment of
additional sums of money. This is especially true if the foreclosure is on
a second mortgage. If you are the successful bidder on a second mortgage, you would be the new owner of the property. However, you
would be purchasing the property subject to, and including, the existing
mortgage. This means that you would owe the money on the previous
mortgage *in addition to* the price that you bid at the auction. You would
have to contact the first mortgage holder to find out if you could assume the payments on the first mortgage, or if you would have to satisfy

the first mortgage when you closed on the second mortgage. For example, let's say that you are interested in bidding on a property that is being auctioned for $30,000. The value of the property is $150,000. You find out that there is also an existing first mortgage in the amount of $70,000. If the first mortgage holder will allow it, as the successful high bidder of the second mortgage, you would assume the $70,000 mortgage payments on the first mortgage after you paid the $30,000 cash required on the second mortgage. If the first mortgage holder will not allow you to assume the $70,000, you would then need to have the funds available to pay the $30,000 that you are obligated to pay as the successful high bidder, *in addition to* the $70,000 required to satisfy the first mortgage. Many lenders will require that the first mortgage be paid off in this fashion, especially if there is a *due-on-sale* clause in the original first mortgage note. The due-on-sale clause provides that the mortgage is *not* assumable, and when ownership of the property is conveyed to someone else, the mortgage balance is due and payable. Even in a forced sale (which is what a mortgage foreclosure is) the due-on-sale clause must be honored. In certain cases, the original lender may let you assume a loan, even if there is a due-on-sale clause, but the rate and other terms of the loan may have to be renegotiated with the original mortgagee (lender). The above-mentioned example would be a good deal even if the first mortgage had to be paid off, because the total purchase price is $100,000 for a property worth $150,000. This is one of the more important questions to ask because you could be in a lot of trouble if you thought you were purchasing a property for $30,000 when you were actually going to need $100,000.

□ Is there an existing certificate of occupancy (or its equivalent) on file?

Contact (or visit) the town hall in the town where the premises are located and find out if there is an existing certificate of occupancy (CO) on file. A certificate of occupancy (or its equivalent) is issued by a town's building department and certifies that the construction of the dwelling was done in accordance with local building codes. A certificate of occupancy is shown in Figure 10-1.

□ Is there an updated survey on file?

Find out if there is an existing survey for the property. A survey is an illustration of the location, form, and description of a property within

SAMPLE CERTIFICATE OF OCCUPANCY

BUILDING DEPARTMENT
TOWN OF SMITHTOWN
SUFFOLK COUNTY, N.Y.

OCCUPANCY
CERTIFICATE OF
COMPLIANCE

This certifies that the ....Building...............................

located at S/S New Highway, Valmont Village, Sec. # 5 ....

....

....

Described .... Map No. .... Block .... Lot No...............

Conforms substantially with the terms and requirements of the New York State Building Code and

Town of Smithtown Zoning Ordinance, as amended to date, and may be permitted to be used and

occupied as a . One Family Dwelling 43.6 x 24.8 with 2 car att/garage ....

Subject to the following conditions: ....

....

....

Owner Melody Construction, Inc. Commack, NY...................................

Signed .....Harvey R. Manuel

BUILDING OFFICIAL

The building or any part there of shall not be used for any purposes other than for which it is
certified. Cerficate will be null and void if this building is altered in any manner or additions are made
thereto without authorization from the Building Department.

Figure 10-1. A certificate of occupancy.

its boundaries. Figure 10-2 is a sample survey of a property improved with a two-story dwelling.

Now compare your pictures from the original inspection you made to the certificate of occupancy and the survey. Make sure that all additions and improvements are accounted for. Sure, you may have always dreamed of that inground pool, and the deck that was added *looks* pretty sturdy, but if these improvements are in violation of building codes in your area, or if they have not been approved by the property authorities, you could be in for some costly problems. In most states, a certificate of occupancy or its equivalent, along with an updated survey, are required in order for you to get a mortgage loan. Even if you are buying the property at the auction with cash and you don't need a mortgage loan, whoever you sell the property to in later years will probably need a mortgage loan and will be unable to get one unless these documents can be produced. Many foreclosure purchasers will still bid on property with incomplete or missing documents. When they're preparing their bid amounts, they simply take into consideration the costs they'll incur for the work that will be involved in getting these documents. For instance, let's say you are interested in a property that is worth $160,000. The upset price at the auction is $60,000. The property has an inground pool, but the previous owners never got the proper permits to build it and there is no certificate of occupancy to confirm that it was built in accordance with local building codes. You call the local building inspector for an appointment. The inspector will inspect the pool and tell you what repairs will be required (that is, fences, electrical work, and so forth) in order to satisfy the building codes so that the certificate of occupancy can be issued for the pool. You will need to contact the local tax assessor to find out if there will be a significant increase in the property taxes once any improvements are completed. Ask a licensed contractor to give you a written estimate for the costs of the required repairs. Get a price from a surveyor for the cost of the updated survey which will include the inground pool. Let's say the total estimates for repairs and costs involved with obtaining the documents are approximately $10,000. If the property taxes aren't affected greatly by the improvements, the property purchase of $60,000, plus the $10,000 costs involved with getting the documents you need, totals $70,000. This is still a good deal because the property value is $160,000. Many people feel that if you can purchase a property for a small fraction of its actual value, then it's still well worthwhile even if work is required to obtain the missing documents.

SAMPLE SURVEY

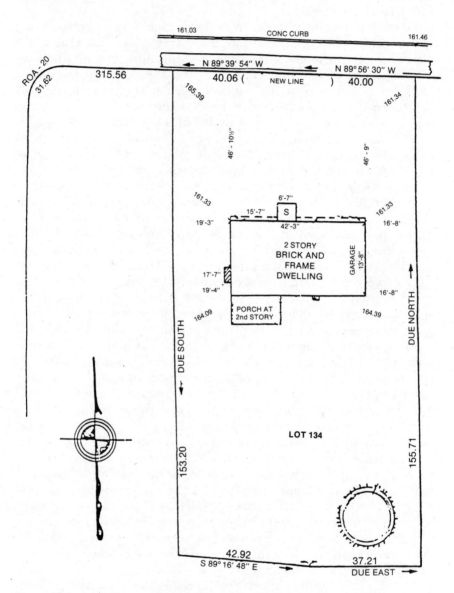

Figure 10-2. A sample survey for a property improved with a two-story dwelling.

☐ Is there a rental permit requirement by the town for you to rent out the property you are interested in, and is there a current rental permit in effect?

Ask if there is a rental permit requirement by the town. This is for investors who intend to buy a property to use as an investment (rented out to others). Some towns require that you obtain a rental permit in this situation. The procedure may simply require an application to be made to the town (or city) building department along with a small fee. The town (or city) inspector may perform an inspection of the property to insure that the premises are not substandard. Because procedures vary from one area to another, you should contact the appropriate parties for the procedure that is followed in the area you are interested in.

☐ Are there currently any outstanding utility debts?

Contact the utility companies that service the premises (for example, water, gas, and electricity) and ask if there are currently any outstanding utility debts. If there are, ask who is responsible for payment. Would you, as the new owner, have to pay all arrears in order to reinstate service? In many cases utility arrears are included in the upset price, but if, for some reason, this has not been done, then a utility company may require the new owner to pay the arrears in full before they will reinstate service. The amount that is required to be paid may be substantial or it may be negligible, but in either case, knowing this amount will help you calculate your bid amount since you will need to incorporate all your expenses into the preparation of your bid. This situation can occur when you are buying a bank-owned property, as well as a foreclosure at an auction.

☐ Are there any incomplete services?

Ask if there are any incomplete community services that will require additional funds. If you are purchasing property with an incomplete sewer hookup you may run into a huge expense if the property has a large set back from the area where the main sewer lines need to be connected. The same situation may occur in areas where well water is being replaced with city or community water services.

In any such situations, if you are able to get the property for a low enough price, just incorporate the amounts you will need to make the necessary repairs into your expenses for your bid amount.

Inspect the File of the Foreclosure Action

Contact the designated authority handling the foreclosure action and ask about access to the files that are part of the action. In most cases, these files are public records open for examination by the public at large. Most of the time these files are stored somewhere in the County Center in the county where the property is located. Files are usually requisitioned by index number. The index number usually appears in the legal notices that are publicized as part of the foreclosure procedure.

Available Alternatives

Many people feel unsure of their ability to get sufficient information in order to ascertain that the property they are interested in is really a good deal. If you feel intimidated about asking questions, or if you feel unsure of yourself and lack confidence in your ability to do the preliminary investigation work that's required, I strongly recommend that you hire a title (or foreclosure) expert to search the records you will need and to give you many of the answers that will help you determine if the property is right for you. Title experts are equipped to handle most of the work discussed here, and they can direct you to other experts who can answer any questions that they're unable to.

In addition to asking your questions, if you plan on buying your foreclosure at an auction, I advise you to ask the foreclosing lender's attorney or the referee for a copy of the contract that will be provided to the successful high bidder. In this way, your attorney can help you preview the contract terms to identify any stipulations that may cause problems, such as penalties for not closing, anticipated closing costs, and the like.

Organize Yourself

You will need to satisfy your own basic requirements when you're choosing the property that is right for you. I suggest that you prepare a checklist to use as a self-organizer. This checklist can be used for each property you're interested in. You may have special needs that another person does not have, and for that reason you will need to customize the checklist in order to choose the property that is right for you. Figure 10-3 is a checklist that you can use as a framework for the questions you will need to ask about the properties you're interested in. This checklist is not intended to be all-inclusive. You may need to obtain additional information from other sources.

Foreclosing lender's attorney (or referee):

- ☐ Will there be access to the premises for inspection before bidding?
- ☐ What form must the down payment be in?
- ☐ When is the required closing date?
- ☐ Will I lose my down payment if I fail to close?
- ☐ Is there a Torrens title or a regular deed available?
- ☐ Is the contract transferable?
- ☐ Who is responsible for protection of the premises after the contract and until the closing?
- ☐ Are there any credits for major structural repairs?
- ☐ What is the status of any current occupants?
- ☐ Is prepossession allowed prior to closing?
- ☐ Does the original owner's right of redemption survive the auction?
- ☐ Are there any additional liens or judgments attached to the premises?

Town hall (where the premises are located):

- ☐ Is there a certificate of occupancy (or its equivalent) available?
- ☐ Is there an updated survey available?
- ☐ Is there a rental permit requirement for the township?
- ☐ Is there a current rental permit?

Utility companies (that service the premises):

- ☐ Are there currently any outstanding utility debts?
- ☐ Who is responsible for paying these outstanding utility debts?
- ☐ Are there any incomplete services (such as sewers or water hookups)?

Figure 10-3. A checklist of prebid questions.

Hidden Additional Costs

When you are choosing the property that is right for you, you will need to know what your additional costs are going to be. As is true for most real estate transactions, your actual expenses are more than just the purchase price of the property. Here are some additional costs that you may expect when you are considering a foreclosure purchase.

Insurance

One of the additional expenses in the purchase of a property is the expense of insuring that property. If you intend to live there, you will need homeowner's insurance to protect your interests in the property as an owner-occupant.

If you intend to rent the property to others you will need a landlord's policy with a different type of coverage that protects your interest as a nonowner-occupant. An investor I once worked for owned a rental property that he had just put a lot of money into by doing repair work. One week before the tenants were to move in, someone broke into the basement and completely destroyed the heating unit with a sledge hammer. The investor was not covered by his insurance. He would have been covered if the person who had broken into the house had *removed* the heating unit, because he had theft insurance. Unfortunately, he didn't have vandalism insurance. So you see that landlords have special insurance needs that owner-occupants do not have. Speak to an insurance expert who will help teach you those differences.

For investors who wish to rent out their property to others a rent-loss policy is recommended. In the event that a disaster, such as a fire, forces your tenant to vacate the premises, this rent-loss policy (like business interruption insurance) should insure you for lost rental income while your property is being repaired. Will this type of insurance cover you for a deadbeat tenant who doesn't feel like paying the rent? Unfortunately, not at all! However, let's say you *do* have a fire in a house you rent out to others. You call the bank that holds your mortgage and you say, "Hello, XYZ Bank? We just had a fire in the house and the tenants had to move out. We won't be receiving any rental income for a while, so we won't be able to make the mortgage payments for a few months or so, okay?" What will XYZ Bank say? "See you at the foreclosure." With rent-loss insurance, however, you should be entitled to the full lost rental payments from your insurance company, which will help you pay the mortgage.

Another insurance expense is title insurance. Again, as in almost all real estate purchases, you will need to obtain title insurance. This will insure you for a good and marketable title and will help protect you against claims from previous debtors. Your attorney can help you to choose the proper coverage.

If you are planning to rent the house out to others, it is best to qualify the prospective tenants and their ability to pay the rent each month. But what if the tenants have an accident and are unable to work? How are they going to pay you the rent? Now you are stuck in the uncomfortable position of dealing with an injured tenant who can't pay you, as well as the possibility of a costly and lengthy eviction procedure. I suggest a tenant's disability policy, which insures tenants who could become disabled and therefore unable to pay the rent. The cost of this type of policy will vary according to the amount of coverage and the tenant's age, sex, and occupation; however, the cost can be as low as a few dollars a month. You can have your tenant buy the policy and name you (the landlord) as the beneficiary, or you can buy the policy for the tenant and be both owner and beneficiary. This qualifies for a tax deduction as a landlord's expense.

If you intend to live in the premises, then a mortgage disability policy is suggested. What if *you* have an accident and are unable to work? Who will pay *your* mortgage? Will *you* be foreclosed on? A mortgage disability policy could be one of the most important types of insurance to consider when buying a foreclosure or any other type of real estate.

Property Documents

If you have found that there are missing documents that you require for the property, you may incur additional expenses while procuring them.

If you need a survey, the building department in the town (or city) hall where the premises are located may already have this document on record. There is usually a minimal fee to obtain a copy. If the existing survey is more than 10 years old, or if there were improvements to the premises that affect the structure, or additions to the premises that do not appear on the original survey (such as a deck, an inground pool, or a new detached garage), you might need a new survey prepared. This may be an expensive undertaking. Remember, there is no obligation for the foreclosing lender to provide you with a new survey if you are purchasing the property at an auction.

The certificate of occupancy (or related proof of structural approval) should also be on file with the town (or city) building department in the town (or city) where the premises are located. If a new CO is required, the normal procedure for obtaining one includes a visit from the appropriate inspector. The inspector will examine the premises to make sure that any additions or improvements were done in accordance with the local building codes. This may result in violations that will require costly repairs. These violations may not have been applicable at the time that the structure was completed, but new, updated services may be required under current building codes.

In some cases if you plan to rent the property out to others, you will need a rental permit. This permit may be required by the local building department to approve the dwelling for renting out to others. An in-

spection by the local building department and a fee for the permit may
also be required. The purpose of this procedure is to protect potential
tenants from substandard living conditions.

Utility Expenses

Additional utility expenses include water, electric, and gas charges that
may have accrued under the previous owner and that must be satisfied
in order to have the services reinstated. Cesspool certifications, well
tests, and sewer hookups also fall into this category.

Repairs

The repair costs include both structural and cosmetic repairs, per the
reports given to you by your licensed contractor or engineer. Figure 10-
4 is a sample engineer's report. Chapter 14 shows you how to hire and
work with your contractor.

Eviction Costs

The burden of removing the existing occupants may be on you, as the
new owner, unless otherwise agreed. This will include court costs and
legal fees, naturally, and if you are buying the foreclosure as an investor, don't forget the rent loss that you will sustain during the eviction
period.

Unpaid Taxes

A property purchased at an auction will usually include the amount of
the unpaid property taxes for the period prior to the auction date.
However, from the date that you are the successful high bidder at the
auction, until the day you close, you may be responsible for the amount
of property taxes that have accrued. This is because the property tax
arrears can only be figured accurately for the period that the delin-
quency began until the date the auction is scheduled to be held. Because
of the uncertainty about the actual date that title will pass, however, the
responsibility for payment of tax arrears between the auction date and
the closing date is that of the successful high bidder. For example, with
an expected closing period of 30 days between the auction date and the

SAMPLE OF AN ENGINEER'S REPORT

I. OUTSIDE
1. GRADING: Good ☐ Fair ☐ Poor ☐ Low Spots: Yes___ ; 2. NO. ELECT. WIRES___ Over ☐ Under ☐ Capacity___ Amps
3. TERMITES: None Apparent ☐ Evidences of ☐ : _____
4. EXTERIOR WALLS: Material _____
   Repairs Needed: Yes ☐ _____
5. ROOFING: Material: _____ Age: _____ Years
   Repairs Needed: Yes ☐ _____
6. GUTTERS & LEADERS: Material _____ Drains/Drywells; Yes ☐ No ☐ ; Repair/Replacement: _____

II. SUPPORT STRUCTURE: MECHANICAL/ELECTRICAL
1. BSMT: Full ☐ Partial ☐ CRAWL: ☐ SLAB: ☐ Full ☐ Partial ☐ _____
2. WATER PENETRATION: Seepage ☐ Dampness ☐ _____
3. FLOOR: Concrete ☐ Wood ☐ Dirt ☐ ; Cracks: Some ☐ Many ☐ Texture: Smooth ☐ Rough ☐ Floor Drains: Yes ☐
4. TERMITES: None Apparent ☐ Evidences of ☐ : _____
5. FOUNDATION WALLS: Material_____ Condition_____ Cracks: Yes ☐ No ☐ Not Visible ☐
6. COLUMNS: Material_____ (Not) (Part) Visible ☐ Condition_____
7. GIRDERS: Material_____ (Not) (Part) Visible ☐ Condition_____
8. FLOOR JOISTS: Size/Spacing/Span_____ (Not) (Few) Visible ☐ Condition_____
9. HEATING SYSTEM: Hot Water ☐ Hot Air ☐ Steam ☐ ; Fuel: Gas ☐ Oil ☐ Elect. ☐ ; No. of Zones___ Vented: Yes ☐ No ☐

III. ATTIC AREA
1. ROOF RAFTERS: Size & Spacing_____ Standard ☐ Below Standard ☐ Evidences of Rot: Yes ☐ No ☐
2. INSULATION: Floor ☐ Walls ☐ Roof ☐ None ☐ Vapor Barrier: Yes ☐ No ☐ Type and Thickness_____
3. FLOOR JOISTS: Size & Spacing:_____ Can Accommodate Normal Storage: Yes ☐ No ☐ Flooring: Yes ☐ No ☐ Partial ☐
4. VENTILATION: Adequate ☐ More Needed ☐ None ☐ 5. LEAKS, Condensation: Yes ☐ No ☐ _____

ROOM: _____
1. CEILING: Plaster ☐ Drywall ☐ Paneling ☐ Other ☐ _____ Cracks: Yes ☐ Leaks: Yes ☐ _____
2. WALLS: Plaster ☐ Drywall ☐ Paneling ☐ Tiles ☐ Other ☐ _____ Cracks: Yes ☐ Leaks: Yes ☐ _____
3. WINDOWS: No.___ Type: Double Hung ☐ Casement ☐ Slider ☐ Jalousie ☐; Material: Wood ☐ Metal ☐ Vinyl ☐
   Wth'r. Stpd: Yes ☐ No ☐ Cords Broken: Yes ☐ Insulated Glass ☐ Single Glass ☐ Storm: Yes ☐ No ☐
4. ELECTRIC OUTLETS: No.___ Wall Switches: Yes ☐ No ☐ Old ☐
5. FLOOR: Wood ___ Tile ☐ Concrete ☐ Covered ☐ Condition: Acceptable ☐ Needs Repair ☐ Slopes ☐ Squeaks ☐
6. TRIM: Wood ☐ Tile ☐ Steel ☐ Condition: Acceptable ☐ Need Repair/Upgrading_____
7. HARDWARE: (Hinges, Locks, Knobs, Etc.): Condition: Good ☐ Functional ☐ Old ☐ Need Repair ☐
8. HEATING: Radiators___ Convectors___ Heat Grills___ A/C Grill___ Baseboard ☐ Radiant Htg. ☐ Pipe Riser ☐
9. DOORS: Exterior:___ Good ☐ Acceptable ☐ Poor ☐ Repair/Replace _____
   Interior: ___ Good ☐ Acceptable ☐ Poor ☐ Repair/Replace _____
10. PLUMBING FIXTURES: Good ☐ Operating ☐ Replace_____ Faucet Leaks: Yes ☐ _____ Sink Drains___
    Pressure: Normal ☐ Below Normal ☐ Tile Repairs Needed at Tub/Shower: Yes _____
11. APPLIANCES: STOVE: Gas ☐ ___ Elect ☐ ___ REFRIGERATOR: None ☐ Operating ☐ Old ☐ _____
    DISHWASHER: Functional ☐ Old ☐ Other _____

For more information, contact Taucher-Chronacker Professional Engineers (516) 766-1019

Figure 10-4. A sample engineer's report.

closing date, if property taxes are $2400 per year, the costs can be cal-
culated at $200. On the other hand, in most cases, when purchasing an
REO, your property tax responsibility will not begin until you take title.

Determining Property Values

When you're choosing the property that is right for you, one of your
primary concerns will be the property's value. You will need to determine the market value of the property in a *repaired* condition. There
are several alternatives available to you.

You can look in your local newspapers for people who are selling
properties that are similar in location and style to the foreclosure property you are interested in. You can go to look at the advertised properties and compare them to what you have chosen to bid on. Compare the
sizes of the lots that the houses are built on, the number and sizes of the
rooms, the properties' locations, the improvements that have been
added, the property taxes, the school districts, and so on. This may help
you to get an idea of the value of the property you wish to bid on, although this method is not very accurate because you would be basing
your value projection on the *asking* price of the people who are selling
rather than on the price that someone actually paid for it, a price which
would be significantly more accurate.

You can hire an appraiser and pay a fee to obtain an appraisal of the
value of the property (or properties) you are interested in. In this way,
you will have a much more accurate report of value, but appraisals can
be expensive. If you are interested in 10 or 20 properties, then appraisal costs can certainly become prohibitive. Remember that you have
no guarantee that you will be the successful high bidder in an auction
situation, and if you are going to submit an offer through any other
method, you have no guarantee that it will be accepted either. Therefore, you may have wasted the money that you spent on the appraisal.

Another available alternative is both accurate and (in most cases) free.
What if I took you up in my helicopter and dropped you (gently) in a
strange town? How would you find out about where you landed? About
the economic makeup of the area, where the stores and schools were,
what the prices and values of houses were? How about your local real
estate company? Will the local real estate company help you? (They may
not be getting any commission in this case!) Yes, they would. They know
that, even though they may not be getting a commission this time, you
may need their help selling a house later on. If you're an investor, you

might need them to help you rent the property to tenants, or you might use their services to buy more properties. And even if you never needed their help, you would probably recommend them to someone you know who is looking to buy or sell property. They have done you a favor and you are grateful. Word of mouth is important to successful real estate professionals. For these reasons, I suggest you contact two or three real estate offices that are in the immediate area of the property you are interested in. Ask them for a comparative market analysis that includes the value of the property. Let them know that you would like them to give you the value of the property in a repaired condition. They will use their resources to determine the value of your property based on the selling price of comparable properties in the immediate area that have been sold recently. You can use the average of the prices you get from the real estate professionals to help you determine your property's value. Most real estate professionals are experts about the neighborhoods they concentrate on. They can, and will, help you with your real estate needs.

Cashflow

If you are an investor who intends to use your foreclosure as a rental property, or if you plan to purchase multiunit residential or commercial rental property, you will need to understand the basics of *cashflow*.

Cashflow is the money that flows into and out of a rental property. Normally your rental income, less your repairs, carrying charges, and other operating expenses, determines the cashflow projection for a property. Different classifications of rental property require different methods of calculating cashflow. Cashflow for small investment property, such as one-, two-, or three-family houses, is less complicated to calculate. Figure 10-5 details the cashflow projection for a single-family

Property: 123 Smith Street, Anytown, U.S.A.	
Monthly mortgage payment	$500
Monthly property taxes	100
Monthly property insurance	+ 30
Total carrying charges	$630

Figure 10-5. Sample cashflow projections for a single-family dwelling.

house in which the tenants are responsible for payment of all utilities and lawn-care services.

In Figure 10-5, the monthly rental income must exceed the carrying charges of $630 in order for a positive cashflow to be effected. A negative cashflow will occur if the rental income is less than $630 a month. Any repair expenses have already been calculated as part of the cost of purchasing the property. The tenants will be paying for the monthly utilities, therefore I have not included utilities as part of the carrying charges.

You will need to carefully verify the details involving your cashflow projections. Confirm that all the monthly projected expenses are accurate as another prebid preparation. Any unrealistic cashflow expectations relating to monthly income and carrying charges can be disastrous if they're incorrect. For example, in Figure 10-5, let's assume a projected monthly rental income of $700. This would yield an expected positive cashflow of $70 per month, since our carrying charges totaled $630. One of the monthly expenses you will need to confirm is the real estate property taxes you are expecting to pay. They may be lower for the present owner due to a tax exemption that you, as the new owner, may *not* be eligible for. This includes veteran's property tax breaks. If you expected your property tax expense to be $100 per month because that's what the current owner is paying, but the taxes are increased to $200 monthly when you become the new owner, your positive cashflow of $70 monthly becomes a negative cashflow of $30 monthly. Another property tax snag may be in the form of separately billed taxes, such as school taxes and incorporated village taxes, which are billed in addition to the property taxes. Also remember that there may be improvements for which the previous owner never obtained the proper building permits. Once you have gotten these important documents, your property taxes may increase accordingly. If you have not considered all of these taxes, then the extra expense will cause a big problem for you from day one. Most property taxes can be verified at the tax assessor's office in the town (or city) where the premises are located. You should be sure to do this if you want to avoid the potential problems we've discussed here.

The cashflow for larger investment properties will be more difficult to calculate. Your operating costs and expenses may include maintenance fees, management costs, and other costs that are part of the daily upkeep of larger properties. I advise you to contact your accountant or financial expert for more details involving the purchase of foreclosure properties for rental income purposes.

11

Preparing Your Bid Sheet

This chapter's aim is to help you calculate your bid sheet and determine your expenses. After you have performed your inspections, asked your magic questions, estimated the value of the properties you are interested in, and determined the properties that are right for you, you will be ready to prepare your bid sheets for each property you have selected.

Foreclosure properties are found in four basic conditions:

Vacant and accessible. No one lives there and you can go inside and inspect it.

Occupied and accessible. Someone lives there and you can go inside and inspect it.

Vacant and inaccessible. No one lives there and there is no access to inspect it.

Occupied and inaccessible. Remember the pit bull and the guy with the shotgun?

We will now examine the action to take in preparing our bid sheets for each of these four conditions.

Condition 1: Vacant and Accessible

Take the following steps in preparing bid sheets for properties that are vacant and accessible:

1. *Get prices for repairs.*   Bring a licensed contractor or an engineer to the premises for written estimates of any of the property's structural deficiencies, and obtain an itemized estimate of the prices they will charge you to complete the repairs they have cited. You should also request an estimate of the time it will take for the contractor to complete the repairs that are listed. (See Chapter 14 for more information about choosing your contractor.)

2. *Determine the market value of the property in a repaired condition.*   As explained in Chapter 10, you can determine the property value through your own research, obtain a professional appraisal , or go to the real estate professionals who specialize in the locations that are of interest to you. For cases in which you intend to use the property as a rental investment and lease it out to others, you will also need to establish the property's monthly rental income potential. For rental properties, there are other things to consider as well. If you will be paying for the utilities and other building expenses, you will need to determine your projected cashflow, as explained in Chapter 10.

3. *Calculate your bid limits.*   Generally, the market value of the property in a repaired condition, less the expenses and repairs required during and after the purchase, gives you a pretty accurate guideline of what is necessary for a profitable transaction. Figure 11-1 is a bid-calculating worksheet that uses the 100 percent value method.

Using the example in Figure 11-1, let's look at how all our inspection legwork and the information we received from answers to our magic questions come into play.

The opening bid amount, or asking price, is $60,000. We have estimated the property's market value in a repaired condition to be $100,000. If we assume the property is being purchased as an investment property to rent out to others, we will need to estimate the expected monthly rental income. In this case the projected monthly rental income is $800.

Next, we will need to estimate our expenses, including those involved with the purchase itself, such as insurance costs, mortgage costs, closing costs, the costs of obtaining property documents, utility expenses, and

BID-CALCULATING WORKSHEET

Opening Bid Amount: $ 60,000

Estimated Market Value Repaired: $100,000

Estimated Rent Income Expected Monthly: $ 800

Expenses:

Estimated Insurance: $ 1,000

Estimated Mortgage Cost: _____

Estimated Closing Cost: _____

Property Document Cost: _____

Utility Expenses: _____

Repair Costs: $ 10,000

Eviction Costs: _____

Unpaid Taxes: $ 200 for 30 days based on $2,400/year

Anticipated Rent Loss: $ 800 1 month during repairs

Other Expenses:

Total Expenses $ 12,000

Estimated Market Value: $100,000

Deduct Expenses: − 12,000

Amount to Bid for Break-Even Acquisition: $88,000

Figure 11-1. Bid-calculating worksheet (100 percent value method used).

unpaid taxes. There may also be anticipated costs involved after the closing, such as repair costs, eviction expenses, and anticipated rent loss. These expenses vary from property to property and can get much more complicated with larger properties. In Figure 11-1, we have estimated our insurance costs (including title insurance and property insurance) to be $1000. There are no mortgage costs included in our example because we are purchasing the property with cash and therefore no mortgage loan is needed. We have estimated our repair expenses as $10,000, based on reports by our contractor and engineer. Our unpaid taxes total $200 for the 30 days between the contract and the closing, based on the property tax amount of $2400 a year. We have confirmed that the property taxes are correct. We have also calculated our rent-loss expense to be $800 for the one-month period that our contractor estimated it would take to complete the repairs.

Our total expenses add up to $12,000. If our estimated market value in a repaired condition is $100,000 and we deduct the $12,000 of expenses, our amount to bid for a breakeven purchase is $88,000. If the auction contract terms require a 10 percent down payment from the successful high bidder, we would bring $8800 with us to the auction. Right? Wait a moment....We buy a property for $88,000 and put $12,000 into repairs, and it's only going to be worth $100,000! Why don't we just buy a property for $100,000 and save ourselves a lot of extra work?

You see, experienced investors and sophisticated homebuyers will start at 70 to 75 percent of market value and then deduct their expenses. Today, 75 percent of market value is more competitive, so if we look at our value of $100,000 and use only 75 percent of that number as a starting point, we now have a market value of $75,000. We deduct our $12,000 expenses and get a maximum bid limit of $63,000. We bring $6300 to the auction.

Many times foreclosure purchasers will bring one certified check for $6000 and three certified checks for $100 each. The checks are all made payable to themselves. This way, if they are able to bid successfully and get the property for $61,000 they only have to give the down payment of $6100 and can redeposit the remaining $200 into their bank account!

Sometimes you will see a buyer at an auction who bids much higher than we would have. In some cases, the buyer may either have overestimated the property value or underestimated the expenses. Or perhaps the buyer is a contractor who already has the $10,000 worth of material we would have had to pay for stored in his or her basement. If such is the case, that individual has an advantage and can bid higher and have a better chance of getting the property than someone who does not have the same benefits. The same thing may hold true in a situation where there are anticipated legal fees and the bidder is an attorney who will enjoy lower legal fees than the next bidder. Any specialty you have can help you get an edge over the next bidder, and you should use this leverage to your advantage.

The foregoing method of figuring out your bid sheet not only can help you decide what your final bid will be, but it can also keep you from being caught up in "auction fever" (where you keep bidding even when the price exceeds the value). This is because you only bring enough money with you to cover the required down payment. The amount of money you bring is *based on the results of your bid sheet.* You can use this bid sheet to calculate your bid for an auction, to make a written offer in sealed bid or REO property purchases, and to write your offer letters to delinquent borrowers. Consult with your accountant or attorney to make sure that you have covered all your expenses.

Condition 2: Occupied and Accessible

In this situation the occupants will allow you to enter the property. You will therefore have an opportunity to view the property and its occupants. The following steps apply to properties that are occupied and accessible:

1. *Obtain estimates for repairs.*   Bring your contractor or engineer and get reports of repairs required as well as the prices involved. You can ask the occupants about any structural or appliance defects or problems they are having with plumbing, heating, and electrical systems. Doing this can help you verify and complete any reports issued to you by your contractor or engineer.

2. *Inquire about the present occupant's preference regarding continued occupancy.*   The occupants are either the delinquent homeowners or their tenants. Sometimes the tenants are in shock when you show up to inspect the property. They have been paying their rent each month and had no idea that the landlord was not paying the mortgage. Sometimes, however, it is the tenants who are causing the foreclosure because they are not paying their rent.

If the tenants look like good tenants, and if you intend to use the property as a rental, you may wish to keep them with you under the terms of a new lease, should you be the successful high bidder. As long as proper service of the legal documents was made when the foreclosure action began, you are not bound to any existing leases that the tenants had with the previous delinquent homeowner, and you are not responsible to refund any security deposits that they gave the previous delinquent homeowner.

If the occupants were the previous owners, you may wish to negotiate rental terms with them should you become the new owner. You could allow them to stay in the property under the terms of a new lease.

If you expect to live there yourself and will need to have the occupants vacated, or if the occupants seem undesirable and you want to have them evicted, you can figure that there may be eviction expenses to add to your bid calculations.

Whether you intend to move in yourself, or rent the property to the occupants, get a feeling for the motivation surrounding the people who live there. One property I inspected was occupied by the delinquent homeowners who were being foreclosed on. They had kept the place in excellent condition and wanted to know if I would let them stay should I be the successful bidder. Their son was about to begin his last year in high school and they didn't want to move until after his graduation. They were very helpful and accommodating and they let me inspect the property several times. These people were good potential tenants. They were highly motivated to remain on the property, keep the premises in good condition, and pay their rent on time.

In another case, I inspected a property in which the current tenant had a lease similar to the one I would have given her, except that she was paying *more rent* than I had expected to collect. In such a situation, as the successful high bidder, I would be able to enter into a new lease agreement with the current tenant for a higher rent and a better cashflow than I would have been able to expect from a new tenant.

3. *When there are anticipated eviction costs, perform your bid calculations with the same methods as when the property was vacant but accessible. However, you will need to add these costs to your expenses.* Also keep in mind any rent loss expected during the eviction proceedings. You should contact an attorney who is experienced in legal evictions for an estimate of the eviction costs.

Condition 3: Vacant and Inaccessible

In this situation, you are bidding on a property that you are unable to get into in order to inspect it. Sometimes this is due to insurance reasons or because the house has so much structural damage (crumbling floors or ceilings that are caving in, for example) that it would be dangerous to inspect it.

This is the least desirable condition in foreclosure choices. You would be bidding on a property that could be a complete disaster. Even if the property looks okay on the outside, there is absolutely no guarantee that the inside is in good condition. I have encountered collapsed cesspools, polluted wells, sewer hookups that are only partially completed, broken pipes, frozen pipes, *no* pipes. It almost seemed as though the people who were foreclosed on figured, "If I can't have this house, then neither can anyone else!"

Your repair costs may equal or exceed the purchase price amount. This is not a recommended situation for someone who is new at purchasing foreclosures. Preparing a bid sheet is difficult when you cannot determine your repair expenses, and a guesstimate can cause tremendous problems if you underestimate the repairs by thousands of dollars.

If you need to obtain financing through a bank and you can't get inside to inspect the property, you don't know what improvements may have been made to the house, and you may need to spend a lot of money to obtain the documents you will need for a mortgage loan. For example, if structural changes had been made inside the house, but no one had obtained a certificate of occupancy, then you wouldn't know about any of this until after you had become the high bidder because you had been unable to enter the house to inspect it. You may not be able to get financing until you have obtained the necessary documents. Also most lenders will not approve a mortgage loan if there are major structural repairs that need to be completed. Buying a property that you cannot inspect first is like buying a car without looking under the hood. Unless you are very handy and can afford to make repairs at minimum costs, forget this sort of situation and go on to a different house.

Condition 4: Occupied and Inaccessible

Properties that are occupied but inaccessible are also very risky. You may be encountering bitter, unfriendly people who will refuse to cooperate by allowing you access to the house so that you can inspect it before you bid. In such situations, I have on occasion been able to gain access to the house by sympathizing with the people who reside there. Sometimes, in order to gain access, *if* the occupants appear to be taking good care of the property, I have offered them a lease and the opportunity to remain there if I am the high bidder.

In the event that you wish to buy the property to move into yourself, or if you do not wish to offer the occupants a lease for any reason, I have found it very effective to offer *moving money* (dollar compensation) to pay the costs of moving expenses for the occupants. Do we just whip out our wallets and pay them? Of course not! We haven't even gotten the house at auction yet. We sign an agreement that *if we are* the successful high bidders, we will pay the occupants after we own the property, provided that they have moved all their belongings out of the property and that the premises are left broom-clean and in good condition. Money is only given to the occupants *after* they have turned the keys over to you. Money may be the most effective incentive to motivate hostile occupants to leave both quickly and peacefully. At any rate, *extreme caution* is urged before you decide to become involved in this type of foreclosure situation. The potential risks you will be taking with unfriendly occupants who may cause significant damage to the property may not be worth the money and effort you'll be putting into it.

Final Confirmation

As a final prebid preparation in foreclosures purchased at an auction, I suggest that you contact the referee or designated authority to confirm that the sale is still on, and that the delinquent homeowners have not gotten an extension or exercised their right of redemption by paying all the arrears. Also, confirm the final opening bid amount. Sometimes the opening bid amount will be higher than the amount that was originally published due to additional updated legal fees or other expenses. Lastly, in the event that you are submitting your bid to purchase a foreclosure through a written offer, be sure to follow up on the status of your offer until you know whether it has been accepted or rejected.

12
Congratulations!: You Are the Successful High Bidder

At the Auction

If you are the successful high bidder at an auction, you will need to finalize all the terms of the sale. Make certain that you know the date you are expected to close and the amount of money that you are required to have at closing. Verify any of your prebid questions, including repair responsibility and costs, insurance requirements, occupancy status, and the availability of property documents (Torrens title, certificate of occupancy, survey, and so on). If you have not already done so, you should consult with your attorney, financial advisor, and any other professionals you may need for assistance in your purchase. If you are purchasing the foreclosure with cash, you will need to confirm the final amount you need to cover your closing costs. If you are planning to obtain financing from another source, your attorney and financial advisor can help you understand the next steps you will need to take.

Bid Acceptance
(of Written Offer)

If your offer was accepted by an REO owner or a government agency, you should make certain that your attorney examines the terms of the sale to you, including the financing terms, so that you know all the costs and the procedure that is involved. If you are buying the foreclosure with cash, you will need to confirm your closing costs and any other expenses you may incur. If you are expecting the REO owner or government agency to provide financing, then your attorney should verify the terms and conditions involved with this procedure as well.

Bid Acceptance (by a Delinquent Homeowner)

If your offer was accepted by a delinquent homeowner, you may need to have your attorney draw up a legal contract for you to provide for the delinquent homeowner who is selling you the foreclosure. If the delinquent homeowner is providing the contract, your attorney can verify the terms of the agreement the homeowner provides. One of the most important things you will need to do is have your attorney order a title search and report so that you can make certain that you will not be responsible for any additional liens or judgments attached to the property. Also have your attorney verify the financing terms you have arranged. If you have planned to assume the delinquent homeowner's existing mortgage, your attorney should also verify all assumption terms with the lender from whom you are assuming the mortgage loan. If you will need to obtain financing from another source, your attorney should help direct you in this procedure as well. Other contract terms should include fixtures that are included in the sale, the closing date, lease terms (or vacating terms), and so on.

Coast to the Closing With These Five Standard Operating Procedures

The following standard operating procedures can be a big help in eliminating closing delays. These procedures may be used for both vacant and occupied properties.

Standard Operating Procedure 1: Order Your Appropriate Insurance

If you wish to insure your interests in the property, or if the insurance responsibility is yours because you will have prepossession of the property, confirm with your insurance expert that you have adequate insurance coverage. Also confirm the insurance company's policy concerning coverage for vacant property. Some insurance carriers will require that vacant properties be boarded up in order for you to have coverage.

Standard Operating Procedure 2:
Protect the Premises

Confirm that a vacant dwelling is secure. If it has been determined that the responsibility for the care and protection of the premises belongs to the foreclosing lender until the closing, become acquainted with the condition of the property *immediately*, and back this up with signed and dated pictures and witnesses. If there were 12 unbroken windows in the house when you were the high bidder, then there should be 12 unbroken windows when you close on the property. If not, then foreclosing lender's insurance should pay for any damages.

If the property is occupied, the lending institution probably will not cover any damages by the occupants. In most cases, any repairs that will be needed after you close will be your responsibility.

Standard Operating Procedure 3:
Hire a Neighbor

Visit the next-door neighbors and express your concern for the safety of your new purchase and for the neighborhood. Since you will be making repairs that will restore what may have been the neighborhood eyesore, the neighbors should be extremely cooperative. Try to find that omnipresent, ever-watchful neighbor who knows at every moment exactly what's going on in every house in the neighborhood. Pay him or her to put this natural talent to good use. Offer a fee for house-watching services that simply involves notifying you, or the police, of any break-ins or other disturbances. Provide a telephone number where this person can reach you at all times.

In houses that are set far apart from any neighbors, you may have to be more inventive. One of my investor friends told me about a method he used with success. On the front door he used to post a sign with a big skull and crossbones drawn on it. The sign read, "**Danger! Poison Gas Leak!**" in large letters. No one ever broke into his vacant houses! This type of sign is *only recommended* for properties that are *not* situated close to other houses. Your neighbors might get very cranky if they

walked out their front doors to see that sort of sign posted on a house
that is only 20 feet from their front door.

Standard Operating Procedure 4:
Have Your Attorney or Legal Advisor
Order a Title Search and Report

This is simply a report by a title company, or appropriate agency, that
will verify any existing liens or judgments currently attached to the
property, and help to confirm that they are cleared up or "satisfied" at
the closing. The title company will insure you for *marketable title*. This
means that any future claims that might arise as a result of actions by
the previous delinquent homeowner would not be your responsibility.
Under no circumstances should you take a chance on closing without
the title work. There may be something in the title report that shows
encumbrances, such as unpaid liens, that you might be responsible for
now or that would make the property difficult or impossible for you to
sell in the future. In most cases, property that is bank-owned or owned
by a government agency will have clear title, although there is no guarantee to that effect.

Standard Operating Procedure 5:
Apply for Your Financing
(If This Is Applicable)

If you have purchased a property at an auction that requires a strict
closing date (such as 30 days), you will need to expedite the mortgage
procedure in any manner possible. Therefore, be as cooperative as possible in your dealings with the financing lender. You can assist in the
mortgage procedure by providing quick access to the property for any
bank personnel or appraisers sent out by the lender to inspect the property. Remember, financing may be delayed if the premises are occupied
by unfriendly occupants who won't allow access to the lending institution. Delays may also occur if the structure or systems need major repairs before your new mortgage loan can be approved. If you are relying on financing from the lender in order to have the funds you need to
close on a foreclosure purchased at an auction, any major delays could
result in your inability to close in a timely fashion. Unless you can come
up with the balance of your purchase price in cash, you could lose your

down payment. Have your attorney review your agreement in order to make certain that you understand all the conditions that you're expected to adhere to.

In cases in which you are relying on financing from the REO sellers on their bank-owned property, the sellers may allow you to close after they have approved your financing terms, and you can wait until you have that approval to set the closing date. Closing rules may vary from one REO seller to the next, so make certain you are aware of all financing and closing procedures. Your attorney can help advise you on these matters.

If you have purchased your foreclosure from a government agency (HUD, VA, RTC, or GSA) and it is providing you with financing, you should confirm the financing and closing procedures involved. Have your attorney review all your paperwork so that you are prepared to comply with the stipulations in your contract. Again, be certain to cooperate with any requests made for additional information that's required in order to expedite the financing process.

Coast to the Closing

Once your offer has been accepted, there are procedures to be followed from the time your contract has been executed until the time of the closing, in conjunction with the five standard operating procedures just enumerated. Let's go through these procedures now, in a step-by-step fashion, taking, in order, each of the four occupancy-and-access conditions that we discussed in Chapter 11.

After-Contract Procedures for Vacant and Accessible Properties

1. *Follow the standard operating procedures.*

2. *Get your rental permit.* If you intend to rent the property to others and a rental permit is required, contact the building department, or other appropriate agency, in the area where your new property is located. You will need to ask about the procedure that is required for you to obtain this document.

3. *Market the property.* If you intend to market the property for sale or rent and the repairs needed are negligible, begin your advertising now. Once a tenant has been found, a lease or rental agreement can be negotiated and prepared for signature. Possession by the tenant and rental terms can begin on the day you close. This will insure you of immediate rental income. Sale of the property can be handled in the same manner, and a contract of sale can be prepared to document your agreements with the buyer. Be sensitive to the fact that once you close, you lose money every day that the premises are vacant.

After-Contract Procedures for Occupied and Accessible Properties

1. *Follow the standard operating procedures.*

2. *Contact the occupants.* Send what I call a "greetings letter" by both certified and first-class mail. Send the letter by first-class mail as a courtesy, that is, if the occupants should be unable to go to the post office to pick up the certified letter, then, they will still receive your notification through normal first-class mail. In the event that the occupants do not respond and you need to begin eviction procedures to get them out, this letter will be your proof that you attempted to notify the occupants of your ownership.

The greetings letter states your intentions for the property. The occupants you're addressing in this letter were cooperative and allowed you to inspect the property before you bid on the property or made your offer to purchase it. Any agreements you made during your previous inspections can now be finalized. Figure 12-1 is a sample greetings letter sent to cooperative occupants.

This greetings letter may be used if:

1. You have acquired the property at an auction as the successful high bidder and the property is occupied by either the delinquent homeowners or their tenant(s).

2. You purchased the property as a result of direct contact with the delinquent homeowners and the occupants are their tenants.

3. The property is an REO and the occupants are either the previous homeowners who were foreclosed on or their tenant(s).

4. You have purchased the property from a government agency and the occupants are the previous homeowners or their tenant(s).

Dear _____:
     (Occupant's name)

This is to advise you that my offer (bid) for the premises you are occupying has been accepted, and I will be the new owner.

I am advised that you are still occupying the property and that you
may be interested in arranging repurchase or rental terms with me.

Please contact the undersigned at your earliest convenience to discuss
this matter.

My telephone number is (   ) _____.
                    (area code)   (telephone number)

Very truly yours,

_____
(Your signature)

Figure 12-1. A sample greetings letter sent to cooperative occupants after the contract has been signed.

After the occupants contact you, if you have agreed to keep them
on as your tenants, you can have a lease or rental agreement prepared and ready to sign on the day you close. Let the occupants preview the lease so that any problems can be resolved in advance. Re-
mind them, if necessary, that they must look to their previous
landlord for any security refunds that are due them under their old
lease, and they will need to come up with the security deposit you
require for signing the new lease with you.

    3. *If the occupants will be repurchasing the property from you, a sales
contract should be drawn up stipulating the terms of your agreement.*

    4. *If the occupants will be moving out, you should organize this ar-
rangement so that you are aware of, and therefore in control of, the vacating procedure.*   You will need to know the date the occupants will be
moving out so that you can arrange to be there to collect the keys and to
secure the premises.

After-Contract Procedures for Occupied and Inaccessible Properties

1. *Follow the standard operating procedures.*

2. *Send a greetings letter to the occupants.* This letter is being sent to occupants who did not cooperate with you during your attempt to gain access before you bid or made your offer on the property. If you don't know their correct names, you should find them out from the mail carrier or neighbors and use the names in your letter. This will help create a more personal tone in what may be a difficult piece of correspondence to receive. Any response you receive from these occupants will help determine your next move—eviction, a new lease, or moving money. Once

---

Dear _____:
       (Occupant's name)

This is to advise you that the offer (bid) I have made on the premises you are occupying has been accepted and I will be the new owner.

I have been advised that you are still in possession of the premises and would appreciate your contacting me concerning your plans to move out. I understand the inconvenience this may cause you and would like to discuss assistance that I may be able to offer you for moving costs or other expenses.

Please contact the undersigned at your earliest convenience to discuss this matter.

My telephone number is (   ) _____
                              (area code) (telephone number)

Very truly yours,

_____
(Your signature)

Figure 12-2. A sample greetings letter sent to uncooperative occupants after the contract has been signed.

again, as for cooperative tenants, the greetings letter should be sent by both first-class mail and as a certified letter. Figure 12-2 is a sample greetings letter to uncooperative occupants.

After-Contract Procedures for Vacant and Inaccessible Properties

1. *Follow the standard operating procedures.*

2. *Continue to inspect the premises on a regular basis.* If vandalism occurs, inform the designated authority so that proper insurance procedures can be followed.

3. *If you have taken possession of the property and are responsible for any damages, you will need to advise your own insurance agency about any claims.*

Figure 12-3 is a basic checklist of things to be done after the contract has been signed. This checklist is not intended to be all-inclusive. You may need to obtain some additional information from other sources. Keep this checklist at easy access for convenient reference.

AFTER THE CONTRACT IS SIGNED, DO THE FOLLOWING:

- □ Order the appropriate insurance (if required).
- □ Protect the premises.
- □ Hire a neighbor.
- □ Have an attorney order title search and title insurance.
- □ Apply for a mortgage loan (if applicable).
- □ Obtain a rental permit (if required).
- □ Market the property (if desired).
- □ Send out greetings letters (if necessary).
- □ Organize vacancy arrangements with occupants (if applicable).
- □ Inspect the premises prior to closing.

Figure 12-3. After-contract checklist.

13
Now That You Own the Property

We have reached the final countdown. Now you are ready to be the new owner of your foreclosure. Pat yourself on the back and follow along with your closing-day duties and the last steps needed to complete the transaction.

Your Closing-Day Duties

On the day you close you will complete your financing requirements as agreed upon in your contract terms. If you have agreed to assume the existing loan from a delinquent homeowner, you will have to complete the paperwork required by the lender involved. If you have obtained your own new mortgage loan, you will have to complete the paperwork required by your new financing lender. If financing is being provided by the seller (as in a foreclosure purchased from a government agency or an REO), you will have to sign all the required financing documents. Make certain you understand all the terms and conditions of the loan. Your attorney can help advise you in this regard. If you are purchasing the foreclosure with cash, you will be paying the amount agreed upon to the designated authority and will be given the deed to the property. You will already know the details of any title problems from the title report that your attorney ordered, and you should have a title policy that protects you against any further claims.

Order the Appropriate Insurance

You may already have ordered your property insurance after you entered into contract on your property, depending on the foreclosing lender's requirements. You will also have had the property insured for the day you close in order to avoid a gap in insurance coverage.

Begin Necessary Repair Work

If you will be doing the repair work yourself or using a licensed contractor, you can begin the necessary repairs on your foreclosure after you close. If you are planning to use the property as an investment that will be rented out to others and the property is vacant now, it is important that repairs be made as expeditiously as possible in order to avoid costly rent losses. Chapter 14 covers procedures required for repairs to your foreclosure.

Begin Restoration of Utility Service

If your foreclosure is currently vacant and in need of repairs, in most cases you will need to have the utilities (water, gas, electric) turned on so that work can begin quickly. If the utilities are in the previous owner's name, as in an REO or government foreclosure purchase, you will need to have them transferred to your name in order to avoid service interruptions. If you have tenants moving in and your rental agreement stipulates that they will be responsible for utility services, you will need to advise them to contact the utility companies to have service restored in their names. The utility companies may require a deposit fee for a new customer, and some may even require proof that you are the new owner. The deed you get at the closing should be sufficient evidence of your new ownership.

Begin Eviction Proceedings

The eviction of any occupants living in the premises may be delayed until the deed showing you as the new owner has been recorded in the town or county clerk's office, depending on the state's custom. If there is a backlog of several months in the recording office and the deed showing you as the new owner is held up for a long period of time, this could delay the eviction procedure. In some cases, someone at the closing is designated to hand deliver the deed to the proper authorities right after the closing in order to expedite the recording procedure (and thereby, the eviction process). Your attorney should be consulted for the proper procedure to follow.

Contact Your Local Tax Collector

Contact the tax collector's office in the town where your new property is located and let them know of your new ownership. If you have obtained or assumed a mortgage with an escrow account for property taxes, then the lender will collect the necessary fees as part of your monthly mortgage payment, and will be responsible for making timely payments directly to the tax collector. On the other hand, if you have purchased your foreclosure with cash, or the mortgage you have obtained does not provide for escrow of real estate property taxes, you will be responsible for payment of the property taxes directly to the tax collector.

Once the deed showing you as the new owner is recorded, the tax collector will be made aware of your new ownership of the property and can forward the new tax bills to you. If, however, there is a backlog in the recording office, there may be delays in your getting the tax bills, which could result in penalties for any late payments.

The letter you send the tax collector's office should identify you as the new owner and should also give the required property description so that the tax collector will be aware of the property's location. Some areas use districts, sections, and lots; other use *plat maps*. Your attorney can tell you the method you should use to identify your new property to the tax collector. Send the letter by certified mail and request that all future tax bills be sent to you at the appropriate address for payment. In the event that there are late charges or penalties that have accrued because of the tax collector's failure to send you the notices, you may be able to have the penalties abated if you can prove that you notified the proper authorities of the information concerning your new ownership. Make certain to send a letter to each party that will receive tax payments. They may include, but are not limited to, school, town, and village tax collectors.

Execute the Lease

If you have arranged for tenants to rent the property, you can now execute the lease or rental agreement with them. It is helpful to review all the terms of the lease or rental agreement so that you and your tenants are in agreement with all the stipulations set forth. Make certain the tenants are aware of the date the rent is due and where it should be sent each month. You will also want to confirm the move-in date and the amount of the security deposit you will be collecting. If the tenants are already occupying the property because they were there as tenants of the previous owners, or if they are the previous owners, and you agreed to let them stay under new lease terms with you, then a new lease agreement should be executed and a new security deposit collected.

Figure 13-1 is a basic checklist of things to be done after the closing has taken place. It is not intended to be all-inclusive. You may need to obtain some additional information from other sources. Keep this checklist at easy access for convenient reference.

AFTER THE CLOSING DATE, DO THE FOLLOWING:

☐ Closing documents should be recorded, as required.
☐ Order the appropriate insurance.
☐ Begin necessary repair work.
☐ Begin the restoration of utility service.
☐ Begin eviction proceedings (if required).
☐ Contact the tax collector(s) to advise of new ownership.
☐ Execute the lease with your tenants (if applicable).

Figure 13-1. After-closing checklist.

14

Making
Repairs
to Your
Foreclosure

Foreclosures indicate a distressed situation. Therefore, the property you choose may require extensive repairs. If you're the kind of person who thinks a "square" is a skinny guy with glasses who prefers reading books to playing sports, and that a "wood plane" is something people used to navigate the skies in the early 1900s, then you should consider hiring a contractor to do the repair work on your foreclosure.

This chapter deals with the concepts behind working with contractors on smaller residential properties. Repairs to larger industrial and commercial buildings usually involve stricter guidelines for hiring contractors (that is, hiring union workers, bonding, and so forth). Smaller property owners (particularly first-time buyers) seem to have more liability because they have less experience with contracting procedures.

Finding a Contractor

If you have hired an engineer to give you a report on the property you have chosen, he or she may be able to recommend a contractor. Or, you can ask friends and neighbors that have had work done for them recently to recommend a contractor they were happy with. You can also look around your neighborhood for contracting work that is being done. You may be able to hire those contractors to do the work on your house as their next job. Talk to the homeowner who is having the work done to see if he or she is happy with the workmanship and the progress that is being made. Is the work neat or sloppy? Is the contractor complying with the time frame originally agreed to or has there been a lot of delay? Does the original contractor that sold the job also do the work? (Sometimes when the work is sold through a company salesperson, promises are made that are unrealistic.) Has the contractor asked for extra money even though the homeowner hasn't asked for extra work?

If you are unable to find contractors through these methods, then you might want to contact contractors who advertise in local newspapers or in the telephone directory.

Do Your Homework

It's important to check the reputation of the contractors you are interested in hiring. You should interview several contractors before making your final decisions.

As a property manager for investors, one of my major responsibilities was to hire contractors to repair the properties they purchased (as well as for my own investment properties). The following procedures for hiring and working with contractors, as well as for controlling the payment for their services, were developed and perfected after many years of trial and error. They involve a system of competitive bidding between potential contractors and the development of a payment plan that satisfies both the homeowner and the contractor who is ultimately hired to do the job.

Broaden Your Horizons

I recommend that you interview and get estimates from at least five contractors. This will help insure that you have a wider range of experienced professionals and prices to choose from. A competitive bidding system also encourages contractors to give you their best prices. Explain to each contractor that other contractors will be giving you prices as well. The following questions can help you gauge and understand the knowledge and experience of the contractors you are interviewing.

Is the contractor licensed?
Many states have licensing requirements for contractors that help codify qualifications. Check with your local Department of Consumer Affairs to confirm licensing requirements for contractors in your state.

Is the contractor insured?
In the event that the contractor has an accident or injury on the job, many states require that they have their own liability and worker's compensation coverage to protect themselves.

How long has the contractor been in business?
There really is no substitute for experience. A contractor who has been in business for a long period of time has had a chance to learn the quickest and most efficient way to perform their work.

Has the contractor done work similar to the work you need done?
Contractors who are experienced in one phase of home improvements (such as roofing) may not have a great deal of experience in other areas (such as painting). Although they may be willing to do the work you request, you would be better off finding someone who has experience in the specific repairs you require.

Can you visit the contractor's current job site to look at the work in progress?
If the contractor is currently working on someone's property, you can learn a lot by going to the premises being repaired to see the work that is being done. Talk to the homeowner about the contractor's work habits and reliability.

Is the contractor bonded?
When there are extensive repairs that cost thousands of dollars, you may want a contractor who is bonded. This insures that the contractor is covered in case of incompleted services.

Can the contractor provide a current credit report?
A credit report will show the contractor's financial position and if there are any claims or judgments from previous customers against the firm or the individual. The local Department of Consumer Affairs can also give you valuable information involving complaints from dissatisfied customers. In cases where a great amount of renovation work is re-

quired, you may even wish to ask the contractor for a current financial statement to show the company's financial condition.

Will the contractor be hiring subcontractors?
Some contractors hire subcontractors to perform work for them. For example, the contractor you hire may not be experienced in all the areas of repair you need and will therefore hire subcontractors for this purpose. You have no control over the subcontractor that the contractor hires. You should ask qualifying questions about any subcontractors a contractor is planning to use, such as their level of experience, what licensing and insurance coverage they have, and so forth.

Actively Participate in the Work Being Done

Most reputable contractors have years of experience in the field. However, it is my experience that even the best contractors are not mind readers. No matter how skilled the workmanship may be, you will probably be dissatisfied if the work is not done to your specifications. For this reason, it is in your best interest to participate in the initial stages by communicating your specific needs to the contractors you are choosing among.

In order to accomplish this, you will need to visit the premises and prepare a room by room "estimate sheet," or bid sheet, for the contractors to use. This procedure will help you to describe your needs and will help the contractors to determine their prices. For structural repairs you can use the report you were given from your engineer. For cosmetic repairs you can rely on your personal tastes. The fact that you have several experienced contractors inspecting the property and estimating the repairs will decrease the probability of unexpected extras that may pop up later on in the job. There is a great likelihood that at least one of the contractors will turn up something you may have missed when you prepared your specifications. If you have not obtained an engineer's report, you can ask the contractors who are providing you with estimates for their recommendations of repairs based on their knowledge and experience.

Figure 14-1 is a bid sheet package which you can prepare for estimates from five contractors you have interviewed and liked. Each contractor will get his or her own package to use for estimating the costs of the work you want done. The bid sheet in Figure 14-1 is a

Figure 14-1. A contractor's bid sheet specifications.

EXTERIOR	Price
ROOF:_____	$_____
SIDING:_____	$_____
LEADERS:_____	$_____
GUTTERS:_____	$_____
EXTERIOR PAINT:_____	$_____
WINDOWS:_____	$_____
YARD CLEANUP:_____	$_____
FENCING:_____	$_____
CEMENT WORK:_____	$_____
SHUTTERS:_____	$_____
STORMS/SCREENS:_____	$_____
EXTERIOR DOORS:_____	$_____
LANDSCAPING:_____	$_____
LIGHTING:_____	$_____
OTHER:_____	$_____
OTHER:_____	$_____
TOTAL:	$_____

(Continued)

Figure 14-1. (*Continued*) A contractor's bid sheet specifications.

KITCHEN	Price
SIZE:_____	
FLOORING:_____	$_____
PAINTING:_____	$_____
SPACKLING:_____	$_____
WINDOWS:_____	$_____
WALL COVERING:_____	$_____
DOORS:_____	$_____
STOVE/OVEN:_____	$_____
REFRIGERATOR:_____	$_____
OTHER APPLIANCES:_____	$_____
CABINETS:_____	$_____
COUNTERS:_____	$_____
PLUMBING:_____	$_____
ELECTRICAL:_____	$_____
FIXTURES:_____	$_____
OTHER:_____	$_____
OTHER:_____	$_____
TOTAL:	$_____

(*Continued*)

Figure 14-1. *(Continued)* A contractor's bid sheet specifications.

BEDROOM 1	Price
SIZE:_____	
FLOORING:_____	$_____
WALL COVERING:_____	$_____
PAINTING:_____	$_____
SPACKLING:_____	$_____
CLOSETS:_____	$_____
ELECTRICAL:_____	$_____
HEATING:_____	$_____
WINDOWS:_____	$_____
DOORS:_____	$_____
OTHER:_____	$_____
OTHER:_____	$_____
PRICE:	$_____

(Continued)

hypothetical example of specifications prepared for repairs to a three-bedroom house on one level (no basement) with two bathrooms, a living room, a dining room, and a kitchen. Each room has its own specification page for the repair work required, and separate pages can be provided for plumbing, heating, and electrical work. When you are uncertain about the specific work that's required for the plumbing, heating, and electrical systems, you can provide a blank page for each system and let each contractor fill out the specifications and prices based on his or her findings of the work that is

Figure 14-1. (*Continued*) A contractor's bid sheet specifications.

BEDROOM 2	Price
SIZE:_____	
FLOORING:_____	$_____
WALL COVERING:_____	$_____
PAINTING:_____	$_____
SPACKLING:_____	$_____
CLOSETS:_____	$_____
ELECTRICAL:_____	$_____
HEATING:_____	$_____
WINDOWS:_____	$_____
DOORS:_____	$_____
OTHER:_____	$_____
OTHER:_____	$_____
PRICE:	$_____

(*Continued*)

required. I have also found it helpful to number the rooms in the house directly on the doorways (with a pencil) when there is more than one type of room (for example, bathroom 1, 2, etc.; bedroom 1, 2, 3). You can also write each room's size measurements on the bid sheets to help the contractor identify one bedroom or bathroom from another. A miscellaneous page can be added for items that are not covered under room or exterior categories (such as the removal of junk cars or other debris from around the property).

Figure 14-1. (*Continued*) A contractor's bid sheet specifications.

BEDROOM 3	Price
SIZE:_____	
FLOORING:_____	$_____
WALL COVERING:_____	$_____
PAINTING:_____	$_____
SPACKLING:_____	$_____
CLOSETS:_____	$_____
ELECTRICAL:_____	$_____
HEATING:_____	$_____
WINDOWS:_____	$_____
DOORS:_____	$_____
OTHER:_____	$_____
OTHER:_____	$_____
PRICE:	$_____

(Continued)

Figure 14-2 illustrates the specifications for the exterior of a property using the format recommended in Figure 14-1 (see page 191).

Notice to Bidders

You will need to provide additional information to the contractors who are bidding on your repairs so that they can more efficiently and expeditiously provide you with accurate estimates. Figure 14-3 (see page

Figure 14-1. (Continued) A contractor's bid sheet specifications.

LIVING ROOM	Price
SIZE:_____	
FLOORING:_____	$_____
PAINTING:_____	$_____
SPACKLING:_____	$_____
ELECTRICAL:_____	$_____
WINDOWS:_____	$_____
WALL COVERING:_____	$_____
HEATING:_____	$_____
CLOSETS:_____	$_____
DOORS:_____	$_____
OTHER:_____	$_____
OTHER:_____	$_____
PRICE:	$_____

(Continued)

192) is a notice-to-bidders form, which you can customize for your particular needs. The following paragraphs explain the procedure for filling out this form.

Property address and directions. This information will help the contractor locate the property to be bid on.

Access to the premises. Is the property the one you are living in now? Is it an investment property where you will meet each contrac-

Figure 14-1. (Continued) A contractor's bid sheet specifications.

DINING ROOM	Price
SIZE:_____	
FLOORING:_____	$_____
PAINTING:_____	$_____
WALL COVERING:_____	$_____
SPACKLING:_____	$_____
ELECTRICAL:_____	$_____
WINDOWS:_____	$_____
HEATING:_____	$_____
CLOSETS:_____	$_____
DOORS:_____	$_____
OTHER:_____	$_____
OTHER:_____	$_____
PRICE:	$_____

(Continued)

tor by appointment? Will you meet the contractors or will you delegate this to someone else? Is your property vacant, and if so, will you give the contractors a key and let them go there by themselves to do their estimates? If occupied by tenants, do you need to make an appointment with them in order to get the contractors inside?

Systems. If the electrical system is not working, the contractors who are bidding on the job may need to bring a generator or some other energy source with them in order to determine the repairs that may be

Figure 14-1. (Continued) A contractor's bid sheet specifications.

BATHROOM 1	Price
SIZE:_____	
FLOORING:_____	$_____
PAINTING:_____	$_____
WALL COVERING:_____	$_____
SPACKLING:_____	$_____
ELECTRICAL:_____	$_____
WINDOWS:_____	$_____
HEATING:_____	$_____
DOORS:_____	$_____
FIXTURES:_____	$_____
PLUMBING:_____	$_____
OTHER:_____	$_____
OTHER:_____	$_____
PRICE:	$_____

(Continued)

needed. Any other systems with an electrical tie-in (such as an oil heat-ing system) may also be affected. Let the contractor know if there has been a recent fuel delivery, or if a small amount of fuel needs to be pro-vided to start up the systems in order to see how (or if) they are oper-ating properly. If you have purchased a foreclosure in an area that has a colder climate in the winter and the heating system was winterized to avoid frozen pipes, the contractor may need to dewinterize the system in order to give you an estimate of repairs to the heating system.

Figure 14-1. (*Continued*) A contractor's bid sheet specifications.

BATHROOM 2	Price
SIZE:_____	
FLOORING:_____	$_____
PAINTING:_____	$_____
WALL COVERING:_____	$_____
SPACKLING:_____	$_____
ELECTRICAL:_____	$_____
WINDOWS:_____	$_____
HEATING:_____	$_____
DOORS:_____	$_____
FIXTURES:_____	$_____
PLUMBING:_____	$_____
OTHER:_____	$_____
OTHER:_____	$_____
TOTAL:	$_____

(*Continued*)

To be done. Let the contractors who are giving you the bids know what you want. If the property will be used for rental purposes, you may have different needs than if you are planning to live in the premises with your family. Generally, an investor who plans to rent the property to others will want work that will help make the property as maintenance-free as possible. (For example, commercial-quality carpeting that will stand up to a turnover of tenants, rather than 3-inch-thick plush carpeting, will be used.) I also recommend that you make it clear

Figure 14-1. (*Continued*) A contractor's bid sheet specifications.

HALLWAY	Price
SIZE:_____	
FLOORING:_____	$_____
WALL COVERING:_____	$_____
PAINTING:_____	$_____
SPACKLING:_____	$_____
ELECTRICAL:_____	$_____
CLOSETS:_____	$_____
FIXTURES:_____	$_____
OTHER:_____	$_____
OTHER:_____	$_____
TOTAL:	$_____

(*Continued*)

that the specifications you have provided are by no means all-inclusive and that each contractor should point out any necessary repairs that you may have missed and add them (and the costs involved) directly to the bid sheet.

If the property requires a certificate of occupancy or similar documentation that the contracting work conforms to the local building codes, this should be noted also. In this way, the contractors will know to allow for the extra time that may be needed for any required inspections by town officials when they calculate the length of time they will need to complete the work.

Deadline for bidding.   Let the contractors who will be bidding against each other know the date you plan to begin the work and the time limit

Figure 14-1. (*Continued*) A contractor's bid sheet specifications.

PLUMBING	Price
(Itemize by room or by entire job.)	
_____	$_____
_____	$_____
_____	$_____
_____	$_____
_____	$_____
_____	$_____
_____	$_____
_____	$_____
_____	$_____
_____	$_____
TOTAL:	$_____

(*Continued*)

they have to get the completed bid sheets back to you. Deadlines help keep the bid sheets from sitting on a contractor's desk while you are waiting to get the job done.

Compare Apples to Apples

When the bid sheets are completed and returned to you, the contractors will have filled in the prices they will charge you for the items you have listed in your specifications. You will need to set up a system to compare the amounts that the contractors have given you, room by room and sys-

Figure 14-1. *(Continued)* A contractor's bid sheet specifications.

ELECTRICAL WORK	Price
(Itemize by room or by entire job.)	
_____	$_____
_____	$_____
_____	$_____
_____	$_____
_____	$_____
_____	$_____
_____	$_____
_____	$_____
_____	$_____
_____	$_____
TOTAL:	$_____

(Continued)

tem by system. In order to expedite these matters, I suggest that you provide a bid total sheet when you give the contractors their estimate package. Make sure you leave room for each contractor to list the date that the job will be started and completed. If you are going to use this property as an investment to rent out to others, the time it takes to complete the repairs is important, since you may not be able to have a tenant occupy the premises and pay rent until the work is finished.

The completion date may be as important as the prices for an investor who is waiting to rent out the premises. You may be willing to hire the contractor who submits a bid that is a couple of hundred dollars higher than the other contractors *if* they can begin and complete

Figure 14-1. (*Continued*) A contractor's bid sheet specifications.

HEATING	Price
(Itemize by room or by entire job.)	
_____	$_____
_____	$_____
_____	$_____
_____	$_____
_____	$_____
_____	$_____
_____	$_____
_____	$_____
_____	$_____
_____	$_____
TOTAL:	$_____

(*Continued*)

the job significantly earlier than the lowest bidder. On the other hand, if you are buying the foreclosure to live in and you are currently living with mom and dad, you may be in no real rush to move out. In this case you may want to choose the contractor who has the lowest prices, even though they may have estimated a longer completion time for the repair work.

Each contractor should list each room on her or his summary sheet as well as the total price for each room. For example, if the total cost for the work to be done on the exterior was estimated at $500 and the repairs required for Bedroom 1 totaled $400, the summary sheet would read:

Figure 14-1. *(Continued)* A contractor's bid sheet specifications.

MISCELLANEOUS	Price
(Use for items that do not fall into other room categories.)	
_____	$_____
_____	$_____
_____	$_____
_____	$_____
_____	$_____
_____	$_____
_____	$_____
_____	$_____
_____	$_____
_____	$_____
TOTAL:	$_____

Room/system	Price
Exterior	$500
Bedroom 1	$400
etc.	

The bid sheets for the other rooms, as well as those for the plumbing, heating, electrical, and miscellaneous work should also be added to the summary sheet. I advise you to recheck the contractor's addition for each room listed on the summary sheet. Figure 14-4 (see page 193) is a bid total sheet based on the specifications listed for the previously described three-bedroom property.

EXTERIOR	Price
ROOF:__Replace broken shingles where needed__	$_____
SIDING:__Paint white with brown trim__ (need samples)	$_____
LEADERS:__Install new leaders where needed__	$_____
GUTTERS:__Install new gutters where needed__	$_____
EXTERIOR PAINT:__See "siding" above__	$_____
WINDOWS:__Replace broken living room window__	$_____
YARD CLEANUP:_____	$_____
FENCING:__Remove left side__	$_____
CEMENT WORK:_____	$_____
SHUTTERS:__Paint to match brown trim__	$_____
STORMS/SCREENS:__Replace front entry storm door__ (Provide brochure for choices)	$_____
EXTERIOR DOORS:_____	$_____
LANDSCAPING:__Remove damaged tree from__ __front lawn__	$_____
LIGHTING:_____	$_____
TOTAL:	$_____

Figure 14-2. Specifications for the exterior of a property using the format from Figure 14-1.

HOMEOWNER'S NAME:_____

HOMEOWNER'S TELEPHONE NUMBER:_____

PROPERTY ADDRESS:_____

DIRECTIONS:_____

_____

_____

ACCESS:_____

_____

SYSTEMS:

      Electric: On Off   Date:_____

      Heating: Oil delivered Not operating

      Winterized: Yes No   Date:_____

TO BE DONE:_____

_____

_____

_____

DEADLINE FOR BIDS:

COMPLETED BID SHEETS MUST BE DELIVERED
BEFORE_____.

BIDS RECEIVED AFTER THIS DATE ARE DISQUALIFIED.

Figure 14-3. A notice-to-bidders form.

PROPERTY ADDRESS:_____

CONTRACTOR'S NAME:_____

CONTRACTOR'S ADDRESS:_____

_____

CONTRACTOR'S TELEPHONE NUMBER:_____

TOTAL PRICE OF JOB: $_____

DATE WORK WILL BEGIN:_____

DATE OF COMPLETION:_____

SUMMARY SHEET

ROOM/SYSTEM	Price
Exterior:_____	$_____
Kitchen:_____	$_____
Bedroom 1:_____	$_____
Bedroom 2:_____	$_____
Bedroom 3:_____	$_____
Living Room:_____	$_____
Dining Room:_____	$_____
Bathroom 1:_____	$_____
Bathroom 2:_____	$_____
Hallway:_____	$_____
Plumbing:_____	$_____
Heating:_____	$_____
Electric:_____	$_____
TOTAL JOB:	$_____

Figure 14-4. A bid total sheet.

Set Up a Worksheet

Once you have the prices from the contractors who have bid on the repair work you want, you can set up a worksheet that will allow you to scrutinize the prices and the work that has been itemized. Look for prices that are dramatically higher or lower than those the other contractors have given. For example, if one contractor's price for the carpeting in the bedroom is a lot lower than the prices given to you by the other contractors, the reason may be that the lower price is based on an inferior brand of carpet. On the other hand, the contractor with the low price may have an oversupply of carpeting from the last job he or she completed and the low price is being passed on to you. Whenever possible, you should ask the contractors who are bidding on your job for samples of proposed flooring material (carpet, tiles, wood, linoleum), wall coverings (tile, wallpaper, paint, paneling), exterior siding materials (aluminum, vinyl, wood, shingles), roof shingles, and so forth. I also recommend that you request samples of paint colors (there are *hundreds* of shades of white). If there are big differences in the estimates for appliances, the prices may be based on rebuilt models rather than brand new ones. Ask the contractors to provide you with brochures for any appliances, plumbing, or electrical fixtures for which they are supplying estimates. Figure 14-5 is a worksheet you can use to compare estimates.

Awarding the Job

When you are satisfied that you have obtained prices for all the necessary repairs, you can choose the contractor who can do the job within the time frame and budget that is right for you. You will need to work out a method of payment to everyone's satisfaction. There are many different methods to choose from when it comes to paying a contractor. Many contractors ask for payment in three equal installments—one at the start of the job, one at the midpoint, and the final payment at the completion. Other contractors want half of their fee when they start the job and the other half when they complete it. Problems can arise when either of these methods is used. The contractor can get paid up front, then disappear with your money (or go out of business) and never return to do your work. On the other side of the coin, the homeowner who is having the work done might not have the money he or she agreed to pay the contractor once most (or all) of the work has been done. Needless to say, this could be disastrous for the contractor.

	Date Begin (1)	Complete Date (2)	Exterior (3)	Bedrm #1 (4)	Bedrm #2 (5)	Bedrm #3 (6)	Living Room (7)	Dining Room (8)	Bath #1 (9)	etc. (10)	Job Total
Contractor #1											
Contractor #2											
Contractor #3											
Contractor #4											
Contractor #5											

Figure 14-5. Sample worksheet for comparing contractors' estimates.

Payment for Performance

The payment method that I have found to be most effective is a system whereby the contractor gets paid on a weekly basis for the work that has been completed during that week. This system uses the bid sheets that were submitted by the contractor which contain the estimates for repairs. Each week, on an agreed-upon day, the contractor calls you with the repairs that will be completed by the end of the week. You inspect the work that was performed, and pay the contractor the price he or she gave you on the bid sheet for the particular repairs that were done. For example, if the contractor gave you a price of $250 for carpeting and $100 for painting in Bedroom 1, and those items were completed during one week, you would pay the contractor $350 for the work at the end of that week. This method encourages the contractor to get as much done as possible because payment is for performance only. The contractors that I have worked with like this system because they like the idea of a steady weekly paycheck.

You will need to keep track of the payments you have made as well as the work that the contractor is paid for. In order to avoid accidentally paying for a repair more than once, keep copies of the checks that you pay and write the dates and check numbers in the margins next to each item on the bid sheet as you pay the contractor. Keep a running total of the job estimate and deduct payments that are made against the balance due. Your accountant or financial advisor can set up a payment system for you that will best suit your needs.

Protect Yourself

The following methods should be used to further protect yourself when hiring a contractor.

Get It in Writing

As in any transaction, I like to get agreements in writing. This helps me to define my terms of an agreement as well as to understand what is expected of me. I highly recommend that you or your attorney prepare a contract for the contractor you hire. The contract should state the amount you have agreed to pay and the payment terms you have agreed upon. Also of importance are the starting and completion dates for the repairs, default remedies in the event that the repairs are not completed in a timely manner, and insurance coverage requirements. A copy of the bid sheet given to you by the contractor should be attached as part of the contract. Figure 14-6 is a sample contractor's agreement form. You are advised that this agreement is just a sample of the terms and conditions that may be required. You should consult with your attorney about the specific terms and conditions that are best for you.

Other Contract Terms to Consider

Default remedies for late completion. The contract should stipulate the penalty for a job that is completed past the agreed-upon deadline. You may have chosen your contractor based on the earlier completion date given you in the original estimate, even though their price was a little higher than the other contractor's prices. If the job is unjustifiably delayed by the contractor, you are stuck paying the premium price without the benefit of the earlier completion date. If the contractor knows in advance that there will be stiff penalties for every day of delay past the agreed deadline, he or she will be more conscientious about finishing your job on time. If you are an investor, you can base the penalty amount on the rental income you are losing because the tenant is unable to move in until the repairs have been completed. For example, if your property has an expected monthly rental income of $900, you would set the penalty amount at $30 per day for each day past the agreed-upon deadline. Even if you are going to live in the house as an owner-occupant, your mortgage payments are due to your lender every month, whether the repairs are completed or not. In this case, your daily penalty amount can be set at one-thirtieth of your monthly mortgage costs for every day the job is delayed past the agreed-upon deadline.

Extensions of deadlines. Sometimes unforeseen disasters, such as a hurricane, tornado, or so on, will cause the repair deadline to be unrealistic. It is helpful to decide what you would consider acceptable reasons for delays, and to incorporate these into your contract. You should also establish the remedies to this contingency. Figure 14-7 is an extension form that would lengthen the deadline for completing the repairs without any penalties to the contractor.

Waiver of mechanic's lien. Contractors working close to the financial edge may use money you pay them for your work to pay for materials

Figure 14-6. A sample contractor's agreement form.

This   agreement   is   made   this_____day   of

_____, 19_____ by and between

_____, hereinafter called the home-

owner and_____, hereinafter called the
contractor.

For the consideration hereinafter named, the homeowner and the
contractor agree as follows:

The Work: The contractor agrees to furnish all material and perform all work necessary to complete the repairs to the property

located at:_____,
                   (property address)

in accordance with the specifications given by the homeowner and attached herewith.

The Time: The contractor agrees to promptly begin work as agreed
to, and to complete the work as follows:

Work to begin:_____

Date of completion:_____

Extras: No deviation from the work or material specified in the
specifications will be permitted or paid for unless a written work or
change order is first agreed upon and signed as required.

Assignment: No assignment of this contract agreement is permitted
without prior written permission from the homeowner.

Subcontractors: The contractor agrees to inform the homeowner
about any subcontractors who will be hired by the contractor to per-

---

(Continued)

Figure 14-6. (*Continued*) A sample contractor's agreement form.

form on the job. The contractor agrees to provide the homeowner with any proofs of insurance or any other qualifications of any sub-contractors who will be working on the job.

Insurance: The contractor agrees to obtain and pay for the following insurance coverages: worker's compensation, public liability, property damage, and any other insurance coverage that may be necessary or required by the homeowner or by state law.

Taxes: The contractor agrees to pay any and all federal, state, or local taxes which are, or may be, assessed upon the material and labor which is furnished under this contract.

Payment: The homeowner agrees to pay the contractor, for materials and work, the sum of $_____.
Payment terms, amounts, and dates, are agreed upon as follows:

_____

_____

_____

The homeowner and the contractor, for themselves, their successors, executors, administrators, and assignees, hereby agree to the full performance of the covenants herein contained.

DATE: DATE:

_____   _____
Homeowner's name   Contractor's name

_____   _____
Homeowner's address   Contractor's address

_____   _____
Homeowner's signature   Contractor's signature

DATE OF EXTENSION:_____

PROPERTY ADDRESS:_____

REASON FOR EXTENSION REQUEST:_____

_____

_____

ORIGINAL CONTRACT DEADLINE:_____

EXTENSION REQUESTED:_____

NEW CONTRACT DEADLINE:_____

Agreed to:

_____   _____
(Date)   (Date)

_____   _____
Homeowner's signature   Contractor's signature

Figure 14-7. A sample contractor's extension form.

on a job they did previously (instead of for your materials). In this case, you could be liable for a *mechanic's lien,* which is a statutory lien created in favor of contractors, laborers, and/or suppliers who have performed work or furnished materials to erect or repair a building. I have heard horror stories from homeowners who ended up with mechanic's liens on their property from material suppliers and building suppliers who delivered material to their homes, but who were not paid by the contractor, even though the homeowner had paid the contractor in full for the job. You can help protect yourself by asking the contractor, as part of your contract terms, to provide you with a waiver of mechanic's lien rights from any subcontractors or material suppliers who contributed to your job. By signing this form, they give up the right to sue you for money that is owed to them by your contractor. Consult your attorney for more information on the best ways to protect yourself from this heavy-duty headache.

Holding a retainage.   Another way a homeowner can protect himself or herself from work that may be incompleted or faulty is to hold back a retainage from each payment check. Thus, in the example given above, in which the contractor received payment in the amount of $350 for the painting and carpeting work completed in Bedroom 1, you would now *hold back* an agreed-upon retainage (I recommend 10 percent from each amount paid to the contractor). So in this example, you would hold back $35, and the contractor would be paid $315. This may not seem like a lot of money now, but if the repair costs amount to thousands of dollars, the retainage you hold is a good incentive for the contractor to complete the work in a timely and proper fashion.

The final retainage payment can be contingent upon several things. If the contractor is to provide you with a certificate of occupancy or its equivalent, then the retainage can be held until the contractor provides you with that required document. Retainage money can also be used by a homeowner to hire a new contractor to complete a repair that the original contractor did incorrectly, or it can be applied toward damages stipulated in the contract if work is not completed in a timely manner. Retainage may also be held for large renovation work when you want to make certain that the plumbing, heating, or electrical systems are working properly over a period of a few days. Holding money as a retainage contingency should be agreed to as part of the contract terms when the contract is awarded.

Additional payment terms.   Be as specific as possible about the payment dates and methods you agree to. If you will be using the progressive payment method I suggested, you should specify the day of the week the contractor is to call you for an inspection of the work he or she wishes to get paid for, as well as the day you will be making the payment. For example, you agree that you will inspect the work on Wednesday and that the contractor will be paid on Friday for the work that was completed when the inspection was performed.

A Rewarding Task

The effort you put into hiring and establishing a payment policy with your contractor is an important part of buying your foreclosure. You have undoubtedly put a lot of effort into the legwork required to get your foreclosure for a great price. If you end up with repair costs that are excessive, you could be eating into your profit margin. This chapter was written for the purpose of helping you to continue on your path to success. Any necessary expenditure of money, as for repair work, should not be taken lightly and your extra efforts will pay off in the long run.

15
Getting Started Today

Follow These Six Steps for Success in Purchasing Foreclosures

Together we have looked at the benefits and risks involved with buying real estate foreclosures. You can easily see that the benefits are enhanced and the risks are overcome through knowledge of the foreclosure-purchasing procedure. Let's look at the six steps to be followed in order to turn your dreams into realities *today*.

Step 1: Arrange Your Financing

If you will need financing in order to purchase your foreclosure, you can go to a bank and get prequalified now. The lending institution will let you know how much they are willing to lend you based on your current income and credit rating. (See Chapter 8.)

If you have built up equity in the house you currently reside in, you can begin the procedure for obtaining an equity loan, a refinance, or a second mortgage, in order to get the cash you need to buy your foreclosure. You can prepare a spreadsheet, as explained in Chapter 7, in order to compare the loans offered by different lending institutions.

If you want to become involved with others in your foreclosure endeavors, and you know people with money (but with limited time to do the necessary legwork) who wish to purchase real estate, you can begin to choose your partners now. You can offer your expertise as your contribution or, if you have some available funds of your own, you can get a larger share of the ownership of the property, as discussed in Chapter 8.

You can begin to build up credit lines by writing away to lending institutions and requesting applications for credit cards and lines of credit, as detailed in Chapter 8.

You can begin taking the necessary steps toward an equity-sharing arrangement in which your role will be that of either the "insider" or the "investor." (See Chapter 9 for a complete discussion of this subject.)

Step 2: Develop Your Support Network

Find an attorney who is knowledgeable about foreclosure procedures to help answer your questions and to look out for your best interests. You can contact your local bar association and ask for a list of attorneys who specialize in real estate or foreclosure matters in your area. Ask the attorneys you contact for an idea of their fees for these services before you hire them. Also, ask for some of their clients' names so that you can contact them in order to get references. It is most important that you contact these clients to see if they were satisfied with the service the attorney provided. Is the attorney always accessible, or will you have to wait 2 weeks for a phone call to be returned? Was the attorney knowledgeable about all phases of the foreclosure-purchasing process? Does the attorney handle evictions? Because the fees and services provided by different attorneys will vary, I suggest that you contact several attorneys (and their client references) in order to obtain a better comparison base.

Find an accountant or financial advisor who can review your specific financial situation and who can endorse your monetary decisions. You may have friends or relatives who can recommend someone to you, and many certified public accountants and financial advisors advertise in the local telephone directory. You can ask for references as you did when you were looking for an attorney. Ask for information about fees for services rendered.

Look for a reputable licensed contractor or engineer to assist you with your repair needs. You can ask for references as well as pictures of work they have completed in the past. You can also contact your local consumer affairs office to confirm that the contractor or engineer is licensed with the appropriate agency and that there have not been any complaints filed against her or him.

Discuss your insurance needs with a qualified expert. Although the fees for some types of insurance are governed by state law, other types of insurance can have charges that vary. With the assistance of an expert, you can compare coverages and prices.

Step 3: Send for Your Foreclosure Lists

If you have decided to buy a foreclosure before the auction, you can begin to contact delinquent homeowners by using the sources and methods detailed in Chapter 4.

If you have decided to get your foreclosure at an auction, review Chapter 2, which gives you the details concerning this method. Send away for lists of upcoming auctions from the many sources listed in Chapter 5.

If you wish to purchase a foreclosure from a government agency, such as the VA, HUD, or GSA, or through bankruptcy courts, you can order the lists of available property in your area of interest (see Chapter 5). The RTC is another government agency that offers foreclosures. See Chapter 6 for details about buying RTC foreclosures.

Chapter 3 will help you if you're interested in buying a bank-owned foreclosure after the auction. Begin by contacting lenders with REOs in your area and ask them for lists of available property.

Step 4: Review Your Foreclosure Facts

Review the information contained in this book on a daily basis—until both the procedures and the success that will result have become a part of you. Remember, repetition is the mother of learning. Review the checklists and the step-by-step activities *and picture your success in your mind.*

Step 5: Select the Property
That Is Right for You

Do a trial run. Select properties that are right for you, contact the appropriate parties, and ask the magic questions about the properties

☐ Arrange your financing.

☐ Develop your support network.

☐ Review all your foreclosure information on a daily basis—until both the procedures and the success that will result have become a part of you.

☐ Send away for the lists of upcoming foreclosure sales.

☐ Select the property that is right for you.

☐ Do a trial run.

☐ Don't give up!

Figure 15-1. "Getting Started Today" checklist.

you're interested in. Inspect the premises and prepare your bid sheet. I suggest that you attend several auctions in order to see the actual procedure and to verify how you would have done if you had actually bid on the property. In so doing, you will build up your confidence as you learn to trust your judgment. (Please note, however, that trial runs are only recommended up to the bidding point. Referees will get rather cranky if you call out a bogus offer during the bidding procedure!)

Step 6: Don't Give Up

No one has ever achieved success by quitting. Ben Franklin tried hundreds of times before he discovered electricity. Thank goodness he never gave up! (And he didn't even have a book such as this one to get him started.) A checklist titled "Getting Started Today" is provided as Figure 15-1. (Again, it is a good starting-off point. It is *not* intended to be all-inclusive. Further steps may be necessary, as detailed throughout this book.)

From Rags to Riches With Real Estate Foreclosures

A foreclosure purchase is a great way for a homebuyer to be able to purchase a property at a fraction of market prices. Many people have acquired fortunes from this type of real estate transaction. The concept of obtaining a property at below-market price as a long-term residence, or as an investment property that is rented out to others, or as a property to fix up and sell at a large profit, is one that appeals to a wide range of today's successful entrepreneurs. Above all, I want to leave you with the knowledge and belief that you, too, can become successful. I hope I have given you the tools to empower you with both realistic goals and resultant success.

Index

About the Author

Melissa Kollen is a real estate professional with more than a decade of experience in all phases of the real estate industry. She has appeared on television as a real estate advisor and on radio talk shows directed at business, professional, and educational organizations. Ms. Kollen also writes a biweekly column for a major real estate publication. The former president of an investment property management firm, Ms. Kollen is now the owner and director of Long Island Real Estate Training, a New York Department of State-approved real estate licensing school with over 15 locations. For information about upcoming seminars in your area or other foreclosure information write to Ms. Kollen at P.O. Box 803, Commack, NY 11725.

Wednsday

Ole Ole Ad -
    price of past ad?
    fax last Ad that
   · Ran

Isabella - 2004 Home
        Expo
      -was Ad sent 2
      us?

Farmer Jack - Did email
     come yet?

Huntington ford -
      -Call mark
      Re Ad.

Aqua Clear fax info/
    call Kelly for Ide.